Private Decisions, Public Debate

WOMEN, REPRODUCTION & POPULATION

© Panos London 1994
All rights reserved

Published by Panos Publications Ltd
9 White Lion Street
London N1 9PD, UK

British Library Cataloguing in Publishing Data
A catalogue for this book is available from the British Library

Extracts may be freely produced by the press or non-profit organisations, with or without acknowledgement. Panos would appreciate clippings of published material based on *Private Decisions, Public Debate: Women, Reproduction & Population*.

Private Decisions, Public Debate: Women, Reproduction & Population is part of the Panos reproductive health programme. It was commissioned and edited by Judith Mirsky, director of the programme, and Marty Radlett, deputy director, with final text editing by Wendy Davies with Olivia Bennett.

Funding for this book was provided by the Swedish International Development Authority (SIDA), the Ford Foundation, Radda Barnen (Save the Children Fund, Sweden), Redd Barna (Save the Children Fund, Norway), and Oxfam (UK). Support for the contribution *The Oldest Contraceptive: The Lactational Amenorrhea Method (LAM) and reproductive rights* was provided by the Institute for Reproductive Health, Georgetown University, under Cooperative Agreement DPE-3061-A-00-1029-00 with the United States Agency for International Development. The views expressed by the authors do not necessarily reflect the views and policies of any funding agencies. The Panos reproductive health programme is also supported by the UK Overseas Development Administration (ODA) and the Population Council.

Panos London is an independent information organisation working internationally for development that is socially, environmentally and economically sustainable. Panos also has offices in Paris and Washington DC.

For more information about Panos contact Juliet Heller

Production: Sally O'Leary with Barbara Cheney
Cover design: Graphic Partnership
Cover photograph: Hamish Wilson/Panos Pictures
Picture research: Adrian Evans
Printed in Great Britain by Bell and Bain, Glasgow

Contents

Preface ... v
Acknowledgements ... vi

Introduction ... 1

The Magnitude of Neglect ... 7
Women and sexually transmitted diseases in India

In Dark Corners ... 21
Illegal abortion in Tanzania

Unwelcome Daughters ... 33
Son preference and abortion in South Korea

Charity will not Liberate Women ... 43
Female genital mutilation in Burkina Faso

The Oldest Contraceptive ... 57
The Lactational Amenorrhea Method (LAM) and reproductive rights

Choice or Authorised Crime?   **69**
    An epidemic of caesareans and sterilisations in Brazil

To See Her Smile   **81**
    Midwifery, health and reproductive choice in Ghana

The Silent Shame   **95**
    Obstetric fistulae in Ethiopia

Double Standard, Double Threat   **107**
    HIV and reproductive health in Thailand

Room to Decide   **121**
    Education, employment and reproducive choice in Pakistan

We Can't Stop Now   **135**
    Pakistan and the politics of reproduction

Rites and Rights   **149**
    Catholicism and contraception in Chile

In the Shadow of a Man   **163**
    Social forces and women's rights in Egypt

References   **175**

Preface

In September 1994, thousands of experts and activists—family planners, demographers, religious leaders, environmentalists, health researchers, women's rights campaigners, representatives of non-government organisations and officials from the world's nations—will convene in Cairo, Egypt, for the International Conference on Population and Development (ICPD). For nine days, they will focus on solutions to accelerating population growth and deepening impoverishment, which is particularly affecting developing countries. Many will urge that limiting family size—women's fertility—is urgently needed to reinforce economic progress and protect the environment; others may strongly contest this. But despite their differences, most delegates will rightly reject "target-led", coercive population programmes and affirm that the cornerstone of reproductive rights and family planning is empowering individuals and couples to decide freely and responsibly the number and spacing of their children by giving them the knowledge and means to do so. Improving the status of women through education and employment, removing unnecessary legal, medical and regulatory barriers to information, and ensuring access to a range of family planning methods enhances women's capacity to make informed reproductive decisions.

Abandoning quotas and increasing choice does not mean commitment to family planning will be relaxed. On the contrary, sensitive and flexible services carry a higher price tag in financial terms. However, unless we meet the family planning needs of individuals in the remainder of this century, we may have no chance of meeting the world's development needs in the next. Notably absent from this critical international dialogue are ordinary women and men— in whose name resolutions will be hammered out. What do they want and need? This book of journalists' case studies lets women and men speak for themselves on subjects ranging from illegal abortion, son preference, religion, and child marriage, to untreated sexually transmitted diseases, female genital mutilation and AIDS. Their perceptions, wishes and needs are provocative, stimulating and inspire hope for all our futures.

Nafis Sadik
Secretary-General of ICPD
Executive Director, United Nations Population Fund (UNFPA)
August 1994

Acknowledgements

Panos wishes to acknowledge the help given by many individuals and organisations across the world in compiling this collection. The following people provided advice on individual articles: Srilatha Batliwala, Dr Oona Campbell, Professor John Cleland, Francine Coeytaux, Kristin Cooney, Susan F Crane, Dr Aníbal Faúndes, Dr Sarah Hawkes, Maria-Elena Hurtado, Dr Barbara Ibrahim, Dr Anne Johnson, Dr Fatima Juarez, Dr John Kelly, Dr Kathy Kennedy, Dr Barbara Kwast, Professor Kyung-Sup Chang, Dr Miriam Labbok, Dr Mallika Ladjali, Dr Claudia Garcia Moreno, Dr Marjorie Muecke, Dr Fred Sai, Dr Pramilla Senanayake, Professor John Simons, Dr Thomas Quinn, Joan Walker. Assistance for the project was provided by Charlotte Webb, Laurence Zavriew, Paula Snyder, Fatima Figueiredo, Heywote Bekele and Jean Bryan.

Introduction

Improving the lives of women and their families is the primary motivation behind some family planning programmes, but others have been overwhelmingly dictated by political concerns that accelerating population growth would constrain economic growth or irreversibly damage the environment. In such programmes, says the Pakistani NGO Shirkat Gah, "it is the womb that is the object of policies, the woman is only incidentally its location [1]."

Increasing numbers of policymakers now advocate that family planning programmes should "abandon demographic targets and express [their] objectives...solely...in terms of satisfying people's stated needs rather than planners' notions of what a society's birthrate should be [2]." They point out that providing family planning services to the world's estimated 120 million couples who want contraceptives but still have no access to them, would lead to fertility declines equal to or in excess of those stated in the demographic goals of most countries.

But women's health advocates believe focusing on unmet need does not go far enough. "To equate the extent of women's stated desires not to have more children...with 'unmet need' for the type of services currently being offered is disingenuous," says Professor Gita Sen of the Indian Institute of Management [3]. Provision of family planning services is only part of the equation for reproductive health, just as it is also only part of the equation for slowing population growth [4].

Services which address a wider range of reproductive health concerns are needed [5]. Governments must also attend to legal, policy and cultural constraints on women's exercise of choice: laws regulating marriage, divorce and child custody; labour legislation affecting maternity leave, wages and discrimination in the workplace; the provision of education; welfare measures; and strategies to eliminate violence in the home [6].

The stalling point is cost. Deciding how resources should in future be allocated is contentious; securing additional funds difficult.

In this book of case studies, developing country journalists expose the human costs when women's reproductive health and choice are insufficiently addressed or completely ignored. The reports vividly capture the daily realities faced by women in developing countries, realities which are often missing from policy debates. Says journalist Ayesha Khan from Pakistan: "Without an understanding of women's subjective experiences, it is not possible to work towards change which would be truly meaningful and desired by them."

"Tunnel vision"

Shyamala Nataraj's report from India highlights a major gap in service provision for men and women—the prevention and treatment of sexually transmitted diseases (STDs) and other reproductive tract infections (RTIs). Even among groups considered at low risk, such as women attending family planning or ante-natal clinics, these infections have proved to be common in almost all developing countries where they have been investigated [7]. In heavily affected urban areas they rank high among the diseases which cause the greatest burden in health, social and economic terms. Only recently have policymakers and planners acknowledged the human and financial costs: "We believe that the lack of effective, coordinated...initiatives for the health of women and their children, and for the prevention of STDs and HIV, represents an extreme example of programmatic tunnel vision—an increasing embarrassment in the light of modern, holistic concepts of public health," say STD researchers [8].

Infertility is one outcome of untreated STDs which is of particular concern in sub-Saharan Africa, where an estimated 50-80% of infertility is related to infections of the reproductive tract (compared to 15-40% in Asia, approximately 35% in Latin America and 10-35% in industrialised countries) [9]. In its statement at the close of the first Population Summit of the World's Scientific Academies, held in New Delhi in October 1993 in preparation for the 1994 International Conference on Population and Development, the African Academy of Sciences lamented the fact that the Summit's official statement "completely ignores that for certain parts of Africa infertility is a major problem [10]."

Restricted services

Unsafe induced abortion is another reproductive hazard frequently ignored. The report by Pudenciana Temba and Ananilea Nkya from Tanzania shows that where abortion is illegal or severely restricted, the poor and the young suffer most. With money comes choice. Temba and Nkya argue that failing to provide safe, legal abortion services effectively amounts to denying equal treatment to the rich and the poor.

Although 63% of the world's women theoretically have access to safe abortion under relatively liberal abortion laws, only 34 countries (including some of the world's most populous) have such laws. In 94 countries, mostly in Africa and Latin America, abortion is only allowed in very narrowly defined circumstances or not at all [11].

As an increasing proportion of young people delay marriage, but not sexual activity, the provision of safe and legal abortion services becomes even more important. Widely supported initiatives to raise the age of marriage should therefore go hand in hand with programmes to provide sexuality education, comprehensive contraceptive services and back-up STD services, as well as safe, legal abortion facilities. The provision of broad services, as in the Netherlands, has undoubtedly contributed to the lowest abortion rate in the world [12]. Without comprehensive programmes, the dangers of abuse are real. Hye-Jin Han's contribution from South Korea shows how abortion "has been turned into a weapon against the female sex". Data suggests that female foeticide has, in South Korea with its small family norms, led to one of the most skewed sex ratios at birth in the world [13].

The power of words

"Few voices have been raised opposing the social pressures which force women to terminate female foetuses," says Han. In India, women activists have raised concerns that—instead of changing attitudes—actions to curb investigations to determine the sex of an embryo simply punish women who are already vulnerable to society's pressure to bear sons.

Son preference has, in many countries in Asia and North Africa, contributed to sex ratios far below the expected female-to-male norm of 105:100. In Egypt the ratio is 95:100, in Bangladesh and China 94:100, in India 93:100 and in Pakistan 90:100. In Kerala, one of India's poorer states, but with the most developed school system in the country and an extensive public health care system, the female to mäle ratio is 104:100 [14].

Journalists Dina Ezzat reporting from Egypt and Hilda Saeed from Pakistan also note the pressures on women to "bring the son"—resulting in diminished choice and an increased number of births for women. Public debate is at least as crucial as health services in enabling these women to achieve reproductive choice.

From Burkina Faso, Isabelle Tapsoba and Lucie Aimée Kéré similarly describe how changing minds is as important as changing laws in their country's progressive campaign against female genital mutilation.

An estimated 85 million to 114 million girls and women worldwide have been subjected to female genital mutilation between infancy and young adulthood [15]. Any discussion of reproductive rights must incorporate the rights of the girl child. Although some UN agencies have spoken out against female genital mutilation, it has not been prominent on the UN agenda.

The right to know

Malou Mangahas, reporting from the Philippines, highlights a little discussed but potentially valuable opportunity overlooked by existing reproductive health programmes: the contraceptive benefits of optimal breastfeeding under certain conditions. She argues that women have the right to know the strengths and weaknesses of relying on breastfeeding's potential for contraception, and explores the implications for maternity rights.

From Brazil, Eustáquio Gomes reports on a disturbing link between childbirth and contraception. Without fully understanding its irreversibility, sometimes without giving their consent, increasing numbers of Brazilian women are sterilised at the time of delivery. The legal ambiguity surrounding this method of contraception and the lack of other options, forces women to arrange for the procedure under the guise of unnecessary—typically caesarean—surgery. Brazil has the highest rate of C-sections in the world, and they consume 1% of all public spending on health [16].

Gomez points to research showing that sterilisation is much less likely to lead to the regret that is increasingly common among Brazilian women, if there is a time lapse after delivery. The same research has shown that "compared to patients operated on by obstetricians/gynaecologists, those sterilised by nurse-midwives had received more thorough counselling" [17].

Birth rights

Midwives attend only a minority of births in urban hospitals in Brazil. Developing the role of the midwife would change the culture of childbirth and could improve contraceptive services. But, says Brazilian obstetrician Aníbal Faúndes, many believe reversing established obstetric training and practice will be difficult [18]. Hannah Tapang, from Ghana, also reports on the struggle for greater recognition of midwives' role in providing better care for pregnant women and improving family planning provision.

From Ethiopia, Tseganesh Gudeta reports on obstetric fistulae (holes between the vagina and bladder or rectum): "the single most dramatic aftermath of neglected childbirth" for women who survive a difficult labour. The condition, says a WHO Technical Working Group paper, is almost entirely preventable and while emergency obstetric referral services are key to its eradication, "its prevention must ultimately lie in a profound change in the status of women" [19].

Where girls marry and give birth young, particularly if they are malnourished, the chances of obstructed labour because of a small pelvis are greatest. Anti-malarials, folic acid and nutritional supplements for young pregnant women can encourage skeletal growth—including pelvic development [20]. But, notes WHO, at the onset of menstruation, young women still have about 12-18% more pelvic growth ahead of them [21].

Fistulae also occur in older women due to continuous childbirth and lactation resulting in demineralisation of the bones: osteomalacia. In India and Pakistan as many as 80-90% of women with fistulae are abandoned or divorced by their husbands because they are incontinent and cannot bear more children [22].

In societies where a woman's role is primarily to rear a family, much of her sexual life often consists of unprotected sex, pregnancy and childbirth alternating with periods of breastfeeding. In unprotected intercourse, women have a greater chance than men of being infected with HIV [23]. AIDS campaigns today must plan for unprotected sex. How can it be made less risky? asks Suwanna Asavaroengchai from Thailand. One answer that cannot be ignored, she says, is tackling the social norms which condone different standards of sexual behaviour for men and women. AIDS campaigns should join forces with campaigns to raise women's social and economic status.

6 *Private Decisions, Public Debate*

Putting choice into practice

Improved education for women is universally ranked high among factors strengthening women's decision-making power. But even this link cannot be assumed. Ayesha Khan's article from Pakistan, shows that many educated women are indeed entering the workforce and having fewer children than their unschooled contemporaries, but this does not necessarily go hand in hand with more equal relationships. As soon as a woman marries the assumption is that she will conform to traditional expectations of a wife and mother; new horizons glimpsed by women students and those who have entered the workforce are often erased almost immediately. And as Hye-Jin Han's report shows, high levels of female education and very low fertility rates in South Korea have not resulted in an end to the practice of female foeticide.

The importance of looking at wider constraints on women's reproductive choice is richly illustrated in the final three reports in this book: Hilda Saeed's report from Pakistan on the politics of reproduction; Lezak Shallat's report from Chile on the influence of the Catholic Church on women's reproductive choice; and Dina Ezzat's report on social forces and women's reproductive rights in Egypt.

"Daughter, please write," urged one of Hilda Saeed's interviewees. This collection is a powerful illustration that while debate flourishes, the new, broader "reproductive health" agenda has hardly touched the lives of millions of women.

The Magnitude of Neglect

Women and sexually transmitted diseases in India

By Shyamala Nataraj

Even an educated person in India, when asked what STD stands for, is likely to reply: "Why, subscriber trunk dialling, of course!" Awareness of and knowledge about another kind of STD—sexually transmitted diseases—is extremely limited, despite their very high incidence.

An unpublished survey conducted by UNICEF estimates that one in 20 sexually active adults suffers from an STD. Very few women are included in such surveys—evidence both of the unimportance attached to STDs in women and the very real problems of collecting such information from them [1]. A recent survey carried out by the Madras Institute of Venereology among 2,100 urban and rural men and women shows a prevalence of STDs in the general population of 7.3%; for women attending ante-natal clinics and primary healthcare centres, the prevalence was 4.2% [2].

Women's vulnerability to STDs—and other reproductive tract infections (RTIs) not transmitted sexually—is increased by a whole array of physiological and social factors. Transmission rates of many STDs—including HIV—are higher from men to women than vice versa. Many infections can occur without symptoms in women, and diagnosis is more difficult than for men. Fear of the social stigma that comes with admitting to this sort of health problem, combined with a lack of acceptable services for women, means treatment is less likely. As a result, they risk developing an infection of the upper reproductive tract (the womb and fallopian tubes) known as pelvic inflammatory disease (PID). This can lead to infertility, which can ruin lives, or ectopic pregnancy—growth of the foetus in the fallopian tubes— which can be fatal if untreated.

In industrialised countries, up to 25% of women with PID become infertile. Before antibiotics were widely available, that figure was 60-70%—a situation which may be analagous to that in many developing countries today, where treatment is frequently delayed or simply unavailable [3].

No way to treat a woman

Four major government hospitals in Madras accept gynaecological referrals for the state of Tamil Nadu. While researching this report, I, too, was referred to one of these with an ailment. The hospital is attended by 50-150 women every day and the service is free. Women travel from all over the state after seeking treatment in their own villages or nearby towns.

It was a little after eight in the morning and already warm. The women sitting on the wooden benches looked anxious and there was no conversation. From one end of the room, partitioned off by a curtain, a voice, loud and haranguing, came through the silence. It was unmistakably the doctor's.

"Spread your legs!...Tell me, where is it paining? Now tell me properly—is it or is it not paining? How are we supposed to understand anything if you won't talk? OK. Now you can go." The woman who emerged from behind the curtain clutching a piece of paper looked bewildered. She motioned to the female attendant and whispered: "Ask her when I should come back?" "Next Saturday or the following Thursday," came the reply. "What should I do until then?" "Tell her to take those medicines I have prescribed and then come back." The woman nodded in silence and walked towards the door.

Suddenly the nurse's voice boomed: "Everybody go and pass urine and come back!" I quickly followed three other women towards the single toilet. Inside it took a few moments for my eyes to adjust to the almost complete darkness. Back in the waiting room some men had appeared. Two seemed to have come with their wives and two others, in brown coats, were obviously hospital orderlies. I noticed their eyes stray towards the gap in the curtain.

Soon it was my turn. The doctor appeared much younger than her formidable tone of voice suggested. As she examined me she spoke in English and her voice was much softer. The examination was quickly over. The doctor scribbled a prescription and handed it to me. "Come back next Saturday and get yourself admitted. We have to do a laparoscopy ['keyhole surgery' through a small incision in the abdominal wall]. By the way, are you sterilised yet?" "No," I replied. "Well, we will do it at the same time then," she said.

"No, I don't want one," I stated firmly. "Why not?" Her tone was surprised. "You say you have two children already. Do you want another one?" "No, but I don't want to be sterilised either." She became more persuasive. "It's very simple. After all, we are going to do a laparoscopy anyway. We'll do it properly, don't worry." I refused again, saying I would ask my husband to have a vasectomy instead. She appeared not to believe me and had a hurried consultation with the senior doctor in the waiting room.

I caught the words "stubborn" and "refuses" and noticed a conspiratorial glance of amusement tinged with resignation pass between the two women. When my doctor returned I asked what she thought the problem was. "I can't be teaching you about all these things," she said, but when I insisted I wanted to know, she explained there might have been scarring of tissue requiring treatment. "But come back on a Saturday or Thursday prepared for admission," she admonished and disappeared again.

The end of the road

Back in the waiting room I met a woman who had travelled from Thiruvannamalai, about 250 km away. She was 32 and already had three children when she noticed a "thick white discharge". Initially she ignored it, but when it continued she went to a "private dispensary" where the doctor prescribed medication without conducting an examination. The problem persisted, so two months later she went to the "big hospital"—the government general hospital. Another course of medication was prescribed, which again did not help. Now, six months down the line, she had been referred to this centre, where she had been told to come back the following week and get herself admitted for tests. "We may have to remove your 'birth bag' [uterus], so get somebody to arrange for three bottles of blood," she had been warned.

World Health Organization guidelines for the management of patients with STDs do not include hysterectomy—surgical removal of the uterus as an appropriate treatment [4]. But I learnt that several women at the hospital had either had a hysterectomy or been advised to have one. "Most women come to us with advanced

10   *Private Decisions, Public Debate*

From polio to "sex troubles and all types of ladies' diseases"—unqualified doctors claim to cure them all.

cases...often the untreated infection has caused an acute case of pelvic inflammatory disease and in some cases we advise the removal of the uterus," said a doctor working there. "Unfortunately, many infections have no specific symptom other than vaginal discharge or irritation. Most women ignore them until [with some infections] it gets to a point where there is chronic abdominal or back pain and then they seek treatment."

Ironically, almost all infections are easily treatable if diagnosed early. However without a programme where women can routinely be checked, most women will continue to suffer in silence.

The extent of the problem

Untreated RTIs and STDs have serious repercussions for women's reproductive health. As well as pelvic inflammatory disease, infertility and ectopic pregnancy, they can cause miscarriages, stillbirths and infant death due to premature birth, low birth weight or congenital infection. Cervical cancer—thought to be linked to the sexually transmitted human papilloma virus (the cause of genital warts)—is the most common cause of cancer among Indian women [5]. In addition, untreated RTIs are thought to increase the chances of contracting HIV by at least three to five times [6] and increase the risk of infant death due to low birth weight or congenital infection. Untreated maternal STDs at the time of birth can also lead to neo-natal pneumonia and eye infections which can cause blindness.

Few studies exist of the extent of specific STDs among Indian women. There are very few female doctors, especially in rural areas, and most women are reluctant to be examined by male doctors. Nurses and health workers are not trained to deal with gynaecological problems.

Some studies among pregnant women show that up to 23% have evidence of past or present syphilis infection [7]. Larger population-based studies tend to show rates of 1.1% to 4.8%.

Other common STDs include the so-called "discharge syndromes"—gonorrhoea, chlamydia and trichomoniasis. But although men have noticeable discharge with all these infections, chlamydia often produces no discharge at all in women and gonorrhoea may not either. Both infections are major causes of pelvic inflammatory disease—which usually, but not always, produces symptoms. Thus a woman may not even know she has had an STD until she finds she cannot conceive. Diseases which cause discharge are more common than those which cause ulcers—but in ulcer syndromes, too, women are much more likely to have no symptoms.

Women may also suffer from other reproductive tract infections such as bacterial vaginosis and candidiasis, both of which are caused by the excessive growth of organisms which can be normally present in healthy women and are not necessarily sexually transmitted. But because they cause discharge, women often confuse them with sexually transmitted diseases.

When helping hurts

Infection can also be introduced through unhygienic practices during childbirth or when contraceptive devices are inserted or removed. Reports as recent as 1991 show only 17.8% of rural and 25.5% of urban deliveries are conducted by trained midwives, although training of midwives is considered an integral part of the (government's) family planning programme [8].

One report from Mangrool, a village in Gujarat, recounts how the *dai* (midwife) "repeatedly introduced her unwashed bare hands into the vagina.... Another woman pressed a small bag of ash against the anus using her heel so that the baby might not find its way through that opening [9]."

An unhygienic IUD insertion can introduce infection. The tail of the IUD may also act as a conduit, taking infection from the vagina across the cervix to the upper reproductive tract. Sometimes women with signs of an infection attribute it to the contraceptive they are using and are even less likely to seek treatment.

Women's lack of information about birth control methods can have disastrous consequences. Says Bano, a woman from Jehanqirpuri, who had an IUD inserted: "The *dai* scared me about the Copper-T so I pulled it out on my own and then I fell ill. I was afraid, so I didn't go to the place where I got it put in. I went to a private nurse who told me there is a wound inside [10]."

Abortions are another source of infection. Most abortions, especially in rural areas, are performed by traditional birth attendants and midwives because—although abortion is technically legal for socio-economic reasons—logistical hurdles make medical services inaccessible to most women [11].

Myths and misunderstandings

Women themselves have little knowledge about STDs and RTIs. STD clinics are visited mostly by men. Services for women—family planning, and maternal and child health services—do not offer STD diagnosis or treatment, with the exception of ante-natal screening for syphilis.

The majority say "white discharge" is the most common problem. Unusual discharge can signify a sexually transmitted disease or a different kind of infection, but many women have little knowledge of what are normal bodily secretions and what are not—or of the fact that there are variations among women. One woman says: "Like every tree has flowers, every woman has white discharge, except that it is not soothing like a flower." A traditional birth attendant participating in a training workshop says there is a separate bladder for white discharge.

Another common belief is that white discharge is caused by heat bursting out from inside the body: either caused by a woman having an inherently defective constitution, or due to intercourse with an alcoholic husband. It is also believed that this heat can be caused or aggravated by consumption of certain kinds of food which are deemed to be "hot". These include much nutritionally rich food such as milk, cream, eggs and meat, which is therefore avoided by women, who are often malnourished already. One woman activist comments: "It is difficult to say whether this is a cultural conspiracy to keep women away from nutritious food or a consolation because they can't afford to eat these costly foods anyway."

Nevertheless, on noticing white discharge, a woman often concludes that her husband has slept with another woman. But society usually blames her, resulting in a profound sense of guilt and shame. She may well be accused by her husband, and the community generally, of having a "large vagina"—sleeping with other men—or, if the husband develops the symptoms first, this again is shameful as it is a sign that he is not satisfied with his wife.

Always to blame

A social worker with the Madras Medical Council explains that many women believe all RTIs are sexually transmitted and are reluctant to seek treatment for fear of being blamed, irrespective of who contracted the infection in the first place. "Because [these infections] are seen as a sign of women having 'slept around', women try to

14   Private Decisions, Public Debate

hide it." She recounts the case of a woman who disclosed after much persuasion that she had a very heavy discharge which stained her petticoat and outer garments. "She had not talked about it with anybody else and begged me to keep the information to myself. I eventually took her to an STD specialist I knew who treated her."

A widely known study in the Gadchiroli district of Maharashtra found that out of 650 women examined in two villages, 92% had gynaecological problems, ranging from painful periods to infertility, and including sexually transmitted diseases. Eleven percent of the women had evidence of past or present syphilis infection, 14% had trichomoniasis and 24% had evidence of pelvic inflammatory disease [12]. However, other international researchers regard the figure for active pelvic inflammatory disease (24%) as unusually high and possibly attributable to the fact that in the area where the study was carried out, sex before marriage is tolerated [13]. The study also found very high rates of nonspecific, and most likely non-sexually transmitted, reproductive tract infections such as bacterial vaginosis, which occurred in 62% of women. In addition 34% had candidiasis. Sensitive tests for gonorrhoea and chlamydia were not used. Anaemia, backache and lower abdominal pain were also common.

Despite the high level of gynaecological problems, only 55% of women reported having a problem and only 8% had ever sought treatment [14]. The major obstacle was their own reluctance to admit anything was wrong. Over half feared being blamed. A quarter of the women felt it was the doctor's job to detect such problems and the others said that since most women have problems anyway, the doctor should assume they exist.

A culture of silence

Women are conditioned since childhood to ignore ill-health, pain, insult and abuse. For men, sex before or outside marriage, often with sex workers, is socially sanctioned—a practice which leads to the spread of sexually transmitted diseases. Nevertheless, even if women become infected as a result, they often do not have the support of family members to consult a doctor—even if they do, social pressure towards passive acceptance may inhibit their search for treatment [15].

Mary lives in Noida, a satellite town near Delhi, and has three children. She suffered from vaginal infections for several years before approaching a doctor who diagnosed her as having gonorrhoea. She was put on a course of antibiotics and asked to bring her husband along for treatment. The husband was furious and refused to see the doctor. Mary continued to suffer repeated infections as a result and eventually stopped seeing the doctor.

Even when, like Mary, women overcome their inhibitions about seeking care, there are few places they can go. In Alampundi village, about 200 km from Madras, I met Pattu. She explained that she had started having a white discharge: "I've suspected all along that my husband sees other women. He must have picked up something and given it to me." It was only when she began experiencing pain during sex that she decided to seek medical treatment. First she tried her local health centre, just 3 km away, which provided free services. She found the impressive building empty except for a sweeper, who told her: "A doctor and two nurses as well as two auxiliary nurse midwives are attached here. The doctor has been on leave for a while. One nurse was transferred; the other still comes in two hours every morning. She has just left now; she'll be here at eight in the morning tomorrow if you'd like to see her." At this hour, Pattu is busy with a host of chores. She has to feed her children and get them ready for school, draw the water, wash the vessels, milk the cow and prepare the meal she will carry to the field for the afternoon.

So instead she visits a private clinic at Gingee, where I accompanied her. The "doctor's" board says "RMP" which means Registered Medical Practitioner and usually implies that the individual does not have a medical degree but only a diploma of sorts. There were only three women including Pattu in the waiting room. The other two carried babies. Hasina, barely 19, had been married for just a year and had a daughter of eight months, whom she was now bringing to the doctor.

Hasina was a little hesitant when I asked if there was anything else. "I had my child at home and the local *dai* helped me during labour. It was very, very painful and she was trying her best, massaging my stomach so hard that I almost screamed. Anyway, the child came out but she had to put her hand in and pull out the afterbirth. Ever since the child, I have been having severe cramps occasionally and discomfort in the lower part of the stomach. I mentioned this to the auxilliary nurse midwife when she came but she said it was all normal and would disappear by itself in a little while. It's been eight months now and it hasn't gone away. In fact, I think it's getting worse sometimes and I find that when I have sex, it is very painful. The last time I went to the health centre, I talked to the nurse about it. She didn't examine me or anything but gave me some tablets which she said I should take every time I had pain.

I don't feel very much better but I don't know who else to see or where to go to."

"Well, what about this doctor here?" I suggested. Hasina was horrified. "Oh, no! How could I talk about all this to a man?"

Pattu's turn was next and I went in a little hesitantly behind her. The doctor listened to Pattu in silence, scribbled something on a piece of paper and told her she needed an injection. Pattu had to pay his fee of 20 rupees (64 US cents) before he prepared it.

I asked him about STDs among his patients. "I have been working here for the last 20 years. Yes, there are a lot of STD cases, mostly men. Women don't come. How can they come? So I usually treat the man and tell him to give his wife the same medicine. I don't know if they actually do. Sometimes women do come when they are in a lot of pain but I can't really examine them and so I treat them on the symptoms they describe. Usually it is white discharge and nowadays these penicillin tablets work quite nicely. So it's not a problem."

However, while penicillin is useful for treating gonorrhoea and syphilis, it is ineffective against other STDs such as chlamydia and trichomoniasis. Moreover, gonoccocal strains resistent to penicillin and other anti-microbial agents have been reported in India, as they have throughout Southeast Asia—resulting in part from inappropriate or inadequate self-treatment of STDs [16].

Poor treatment for men too

The gender divide in STD services means women's chances of treatment are largely dependent on the awareness and honesty of their partners—but services for men leave a lot to be desired too.

I met Raja, a young man of about 25 years old, at a government hospital STD clinic in Madras. He had just been examined. After complaining of burning and itching in his penis a year before, he had bought himself a course of penicillin from the local chemist, which may or may not have been the appropriate treatment. The symptoms disappeared for a while; later they returned with greater intensity, which could have meant a new infection, and he found it hard to report to work.

He went to a doctor who prescribed a course of treatment without examining him or carrying out tests. When lesions started to appear on his body he came to the government hospital. His encounter with the doctors left him even more depressed. "They asked me to strip in the room in full view of at least three other people, one of whom was a woman. Then the doctor called some of his juniors and they all crowded around me. I was most embarrassed and ashamed. All they seemed to want to know was whom I had slept with and when."

When I spoke to the doctors they shrugged off the obvious embarrassment of their patient. "These fellows don't feel any shame. After all, their lifestyle is also quite coarse. They just get drunk, sleep around with any woman they can and pick up an STD. What is the need for special treatment? Anyway, now we have a counsellor who comes in from a voluntary organisation. Why don't you talk with her?"

When the counsellor met Raja she explained the treatment he was to follow, insisted he should always use a condom during sex and, when he nervously confessed he had not used one before, explained what he had to do and how it would protect him. Clutching her parting gift of a packet of lubricated condoms, Raja looked distinctly more relieved when he left the clinic.

The counsellor, who attends to nearly 15 patients every day, says the difference counselling can make is remarkable. If a man feels ashamed, then he is more reluctant to tell his wife to have treatment—especially if she appears to have no symptoms. He usually does not realise that it is quite likely she still has the infection—or what the consequences could be. "Most patients are men. Women come in only when they are brought by their husbands. Usually the woman doesn't know what's wrong and for me, it's a case of [either] violating the confidentiality of her husband...or informing her of her own health problem.... I usually seek a compromise. If the husband is emphatic that his wife should not know, then I tell her she has picked up an infection which needs to be taken care of. I also talk to her about the possible sources of the infection and leave her to arrive at the conclusions. I know this is unfair to the woman but my hands are bound." With counselling, patients are more likely to complete a course of treatment. Numbers attending are rising, partly because of former patients recommending the service to their friends.

AIDS: time is running out

The fact that levels of STD infection are high in India indicates high levels of unprotected sex, which in turn means Indian women are highly vulnerable to HIV infection. Moreover, a number of STDs actually increase the risk of HIV transmission.

In HIV prevention efforts there is inevitably a tension between concentrating on the need to prevent infections on a daily basis and

18   Private Decisions, Public Debate

Existing family planning facilities could provide a broader range of reproductive health services.

giving priority to lessening women's subordination so that they have more control over their own reproductive health. Policy makers advocate effective STD treatment services—usually targeted at commercial sex workers and male clients—and safer sex, including the use of condoms. But they are also faced with the inevitability of the woman having to ask the man to change his behaviour or use a condom and his refusal to do so, as well as the vulnerability of a monogamous married woman who may not even know if she faces a risk because of her husband's behaviour.

But women can and do demand safer sexual behaviour. Prostitutes, who are still widely regarded as being unable to demand condom use by clients, have a considerable ability to protect themselves from STDs, including HIV, by exercising control over their clients' behaviour. But for this to happen, HIV prevention and control programmes must recognise that women will adopt protective behaviour when they believe it is important for them—and when they are given the appropriate information and resources.

Feminists are now questioning the priorities of the massively publicised National AIDS Control Programme. Despite the large allocations made to the programme, in contrast to support for women's health, there is very little in the programme plan that addresses itself specifically to the issue of STDs and HIV/AIDS among Indian women. Similarly, most women activists point out that the Family Welfare Programme, encompassing both maternal and child health and contraceptive services, has failed to address the key issues of RTIs and STDs and is poorly placed to take on HIV prevention and control campaigns.

A safe space for women

If issues of sexual and reproductive health are to be resolved women need to be able to articulate their experiences and anxieties. For this a "safe space" may need to be created.

A recent event organised by women for women achieved just this. An exhibition and workshop on women and health was put on by the People's Science Movement, Medico Friends' Circle and the Vidgyan Sangatana in the state of Maharashtra and received a tremendous response from women's groups. The women were able to share their experiences and feelings, finding much commonality, irrespective of their educational, caste or class background.

The grassroots organisation, Social Action for Rural and Tribal Inhabitants of India (SARTHI), was created in 1980 and works in Panchmahals district of Gujarat state. Its women's health programme has taken on issues relating to gynaecology, psychology, and violence and exploitation, and has trained women health workers as "barefoot gynaecologists" to help local women whose needs are not met by the standard health care facilities.

These workers are trained to do pelvic and vaginal examinations, in order to diagnose common problems, and taught how to take a complete history of medical and stress-causing life events. Women in the area now say they feel more confident in recognising what is normal and what is an abnormal symptom. They are assured of follow-up treatments and in many cases have brought their partners along [17].

Women activists say that the narrow goal of fertility reduction, which has dominated government family planning policy, is inappropriate. As part of an alternative policy framework, they have proposed an integrated "women's health" programme encompassing family planning, mother and child care, and reproductive health, and have called for the government to provide these services through its elaborate healthcare network.

But can the government change its approach, from "number-crunching" to equity concerns? According to activist Mirai Chatterjee, coordinator of the Self-Employed Women's Association in Ahmedabad, the women's movement is raising uncomfortable questions about India's family planning programme.

Is "family planning"—or "family welfare"—really a euphemism for population control? Or does it represent a genuine concern for women's health, fertility and empowerment? asks Chatterjee [18]. The grim statistics on untreated STDs among Indian women suggest that her wish for a wider agenda has yet to be fulfilled.

In Dark Corners

Illegal abortion in Tanzania

By Pudenciana Temba and Ananilea Nkya

"I survived by chance after I had an abortion done by a man in someone's home...," says a 15-year-old girl from Kimara area in Dar es Salaam. "After missing my periods for two consecutive months I told my boyfriend—a *Daladala* [city bus] conductor—who told me since I was a school girl I should not go on with the pregnancy. I agreed. 'You should not reveal it to your family,' he insisted. After four days my boyfriend came and told me that he had arranged with a doctor to terminate my pregnancy and that it was going to be done over the weekend. On Friday afternoon after classes he picked me up from the school gate and we boarded a taxi to an area where I had never been. We walked for a while through a narrow dark path and finally ended up in a small house. My boyfriend introduced me to the man who took me into a bedroom and gave me some tablets. He told me to lie on the bed and gave me an injection which made me lose consciousness. After some time I was conscious again and my stomach was aching. He told me that I was now OK—my two-months-plus pregnancy had been removed. I was happy. 'Don't reveal this to anybody,' the man warned me. 'If you rest properly over the weekend you should be OK for school on Monday...right? Bye bye and good luck.'

"That week my sister was up country. Only three of us were at home, myself and two housemaids. Over the weekend I had heavy bleeding and Monday I was so weak I couldn't go to school. My sister came back that afternoon and finding me deadly sick, asked what had happened. I didn't disclose. She took me to Mwananyamala

Hospital. A doctor who examined me asked what I had done. 'Nothing,' I replied. *'Umetoa mimba wewe,'* she said, meaning: 'You had an abortion.' I kept quiet. Thank God, immediately I was sent to theatre and my uterus was examined. After two weeks in hospital my health improved. Before I was discharged a nurse told me, 'You are very lucky, you would have died...go but be careful young girl, OK?'"

Weekend abortions

"Believe me, abortion is taking place in dark corners in this country. It is amazing the cases of incomplete abortion we receive in this hospital every day," says Dr Ramadhani Lodi, in charge of the Gynaecology and Obstetric Department at Temeke Hospital, a government hospital in Dar es Salaam.

It is commonplace for desperate Tanzanian women—particularly the young, ill-informed and poor—to resort to illegal abortions outside the health care system. In Dar es Salaam, 20% of those admitted to four public hospitals with abortion problems were still pursuing their primary or secondary education [1].

"We record more of these cases over the weekends and school holidays. That is why we tend to believe that they are induced," says Dr Margareth Nyambo, chief gynaecologist and obstetrician at Amana Hospital, a government hospital in Dar es Salaam.

In Tanzania, abortion is a criminal offence except in very narrow circumstances—if it is performed by a physician to protect the health and life of the mother, in cases of foetal malformation or of rape or incest. Under the 1965 Penal Code, a woman who terminates an unwanted pregnancy can be imprisoned for seven years, while a person who performs an abortion is liable to 14 years' imprisonment. Anyone found guilty of supplying drugs which could cause an abortion can be jailed for three years.

Between 1989 and 1991, there were six prosecutions for abortion offences in the Dar es Salaam courts. In all the cases, the accused were teenage girls. They and the practitioners were freed because of lack of evidence.

Contraception: "I don't know what it is"

The question of abortion needs to be placed in the context of women's overall access to health care and their status in society. Increasing numbers of women—single mothers, separated women and widows—are heads of households. The struggle against poverty and the stigma attached to single motherhood make the prospect of bringing up children alone a daunting one. Two-thirds of Tanzanians are Muslims or Christians. Both religions, particularly Christianity, condemn abortion, a situation which has created much fear among women with unwanted pregnancies.

Modern contraception has been legally available in Tanzania since 1959, but many women have very limited or no access at all. Until recently, only married women were permitted to use family planning services. In 1989, the Ministry of Health redefined eligibility to include any adult irrespective of marital status, but services were limited to couples or women with at least one child. By 1992, only 10% of women of child-bearing age used modern contraception: most depended on traditional methods to lessen the likelihood of pregnancy—restricting sexual intercourse to "safe days" or relying on the protective effect of breastfeeding. In December 1992, the government endorsed a population policy which extended contraception provision to all those, including school children, who can "become pregnant or cause pregnancy".

Improved family planning information and services would reduce the number of deaths caused by illegal abortion, says Dr Luhino, a government family planning official. "Maternal mortality in Tanzania could be reduced by between 20% to 25% if all people who needed family planning could get it," he says. But current provision falls far short of need.

Poor provision of contraception, coupled with the official exclusion of sex education from school curricula, results in a considerable number of young girls becoming pregnant. Ministry of Education and Culture statistics for 1992 show that 5% of schoolgirls drop out or are expelled due to pregnancy. "When I was expelled from school I was 12 years old. Teachers told me I was pregnant, but I didn't know what pregnancy was," says a girl at the UMATI (Family Planning Association of Tanzania) Youth Rehabilitation Centre in Dar es Salaam, which offers primary education and vocational training to female students who drop out due to pregnancy. Asked why she did not use a contraceptive device, another student says: "I don't know what it is and I have not seen one." Many girls and women are similarly uninformed: some reject contraceptives because they fear they will cause cancer.

Most girls at the centre say that fear prevented them from having an abortion. "After Zaina's death, I swore that I would keep the baby regardless of all the problems I would face," says one student expelled

24   *Private Decisions, Public Debate*

Lack of contraceptive services for young people leads to high rates of drop-out from further education.

from primary school at the age of 14, remembering a friend who died after an abortion. Others say they would resort to termination if they had access to safe means.

At Kinondoni Secondary School in Dar es Salaam, 30 students of different ages were asked what they would do if they became pregnant while still at school. Twenty-five said that if they could gain access to an abortion they would, to avoid being expelled. "I know being expelled from school would be the beginning of a miserable life," said one.

Secrecy and fear

Some young women are rejected by parents and relatives and lose social support if they are single and have a baby. Regarded as immoral and "a bad omen", they find it difficult to marry. "I decided to abort because I was not married and I did not want to to be seen as a prostitute," says a 16-year-old from the village of Mungushi, Kilimanjaro region. For those still at school the expulsion that inevitably follows pregnancy greatly limits their future options. It can also lead to "baby dumping" and the deaths of the unwanted children, according to press reports.

Women who become pregnant unintentionally are frequently afraid to tell their family and friends of their plight.

"There was no way I could keep it because my father would kill me. I still depend on him for everything and worse still the man responsible, who is about my father's age [45 years], is married and told me to abort because he cannot marry me," says a 19-year-old from Manzese area in Dar es Salaam.

A 1992 study of 455 women admitted to public hospitals in Dar es Salaam for complications arising from induced abortion revealed that almost one-third of adolescent girls reported male partners aged 45 years or over [2]. "This is not surprising", say the researchers, "given the existence of the `sugar daddy' phenomenon in African cities." Economic necessity drives many of these relationships. Some girls say their parents are too poor to meet their children's basic daily requirements. "I live five kilometres from school, and my father gives me only 40 shillings [about 8 US cents] daily for school use," says Mwajuma Saidi, a student at Msasani Primary School in Dar es Salaam. Instead of taking the bus, she walks to school so that she can use the money to buy lunch.

"I got the pregnancy by another man and I felt it would definitely risk my marriage," laments a 32-year-old woman with two children, who ended up spending two months at Tanzania Occupational Health Hospital after she had inserted a sharp stick in her vagina which damaged her uterus and intestine very badly. "I had to induce it by myself using a piece of wood because I had no money. I was trying to hide it from my husband by telling him I was having severe menstruation pains, but after a week at home I sensed I was going to die. I decided to go to hospital where after being admitted for one week and having an operation, my husband suspected something fishy and demanded to know why [there was] such a big bill and long hospitalisation. The doctor told him and that was the last I saw of him. After discharge from hospital I found my *taleka* [divorce]."

Under Tanzania's child custody laws, a mother is allowed to keep a child after divorce only if it is under eight years of age. After this, the father is lawfully the custodian of the child. A mother with custody of a child is entitled to a monthly maintenance allowance of only 100 Tanzanian shillings (about 20 US cents) from the father. The law makes divorce a fearful prospect for many women.

Women from all walks of life resort to induced illegal abortion. "I have seen wives of even big shots coming here to seek humane treatment after unsafely performed abortions," says a gynaecologist at Muhimbili Hospital in Dar es Salaam who asks not to be named.

But for most women who seek an abortion, poverty is a crucial factor. "I decided to abort because I was already a single parent and it was not possible financially to add on another child at this particular time. My son depends entirely on me. Myself, I've no support from anyone.... The man who made me pregnant earns 5,000 shillings [US$10] a month," says a fishmonger from Mikoroshini area in Dar es Salaam. Food for her household—the child, a helper and herself—costs a minimum of 600 shillings (US$1.50) daily and uses up almost all her small profits.

Complications and consequences

"About a fifth of all maternal deaths in hospitals are due to complications of induced abortion," says Professor Malise Kaisi, a leading gynaecologist at the Muhimbili Medical Centre, Tanzania's main referral hospital. "However, this is believed to be grossly inaccurate as it often does not take into account the deaths due to drug poisoning."

Professor Kaisi states that pregnancy-related complications account for the deaths of over 5,000 women annually (WHO figures are 2,000-4,000), but he also points out that mortality rates fail to reveal the full magnitude of the problem: "Deaths constitute the tip of the iceberg. The major part of the problem lies in the morbidity—the ailing, the suffering, the condemnation and rejection and the long-term sequels of abortion."

Dr Matingas, a gynaecologist at Dar Group Hospital, notes an increasing incidence of "more traumatic or radical measures" taken to terminate pregnancy. "We have witnessed the uterus torn into pieces. Some victims' intestines were perforated and some lost their uterus," he says. Survivors may be unable to carry a future pregnancy to term.

Permanent infertility has been the consequence of induced abortion for a former student at the Dar es Salaam School of Accountancy. "I was a student so I was concerned with education," she says, explaining why she terminated her pregnancy.

According to gynaecologist Dr Almansa of Mwananyamala Hospital: "Sixty percent of all gynaecological problems we attend annually are related to incomplete abortion." All government hospitals in the city report similar figures.

Private hospitals report fewer cases, probably because few women can afford their treatment fees, but numbers are increasing every year. Even village dispensaries are well aware of the tide of desperate women. At Chanika village, over 60 km from Dar es Salaam, between five and 10 cases of incomplete abortions are attended annually. "Last year we had about 10 cases," says Expedit Ibiya, a rural medical assistant in charge of Chanika dispensary. "Some of those cases were complicated, so we referred them to Amana Hospital in the city."

Public remedies for private ills

Abortions are sometimes performed illicitly—as "private" work for which they charge fees—by qualified and unqualified health personnel. Public facilities provide treatment when complications arise. "And these young women tend to believe that everyone working in the health system is a qualified doctor who can perform abortion," says Dr Nyambo from Amana Hospital in Dar es Salaam.

Some traditional practitioners and others with no medical knowledge who attempt to induce abortions are aware of the health risks. "The person who did my abortion advised me to go to hospital immediately after the abortion and said that I should not tell the truth that I had an induced abortion. Instead I should insist that the abortion was spontaneous," says a 20-year-old admitted to Temeke District Hospital in Dar es Salaam region after taking highly toxic herbs, often used by traditional practitioners to procure abortions.

However, many young women die because they have no access to hospital treatment after an unsafe abortion. "I lost my only daughter—21 years old—after she had an abortion performed by a traditional practitioner from a nearby village," says a 53-year-old woman from Nronga village, in Kilimanjaro region. "At first she told me she had drunk *mbege* [local brew] which was not well prepared. She went to a nearby clinic where she was given treatment for food poisoning. However, three days later she complained of severe stomach pains, fever and headache. I rushed her to Machame Hospital where it was discovered that she had had an unsafe abortion in which her intestine was seriously damaged and she did not get timely treatment. She died after spending only one night in that hospital."

A common practice, particularly among schoolgirls, is to try to induce abortion by taking a high dose of Chloroquine tablets. Professor Kaisi explains that women have "the wrong impression" that chloroquine is an abortifacient "dating back to the days when quinine was not prescribed to pregnant women as it was thought to be the cause of miscarriage among those with acute malaria". Of the 50 people who died of Chloroquine overdoses in Tanzania in 1989, 30 were women attempting to abort [3]. The mother of a 15-year-old girl in Keryo village in Kilimanjaro region explains that this is how her daughter died, after a mob rape had resulted in pregnancy. "We did not know that our daughter was raped or that she was pregnant until after she died. Her classmates told us."

"We should break the silence about abortion," Professor Kaisi insists. "People, young girls in particular, should be enlightened that Chloroquine does not cause abortion. It kills the mother before abortion occurs."

A gynaecologist at Muhimbili Hospital says: "We should not pretend that abortion is not taking place while doctors in both government and private hospitals are always busy treating women with complications resulting from abortions done outside hospitals and sometimes by quacks."

Health experts believe that in countries with legal restrictions, abortion risks can be drastically reduced by timely access to professional medical treatment [4].

Safety at a price

Some private hospitals in Dar es Salaam are prepared to terminate unwanted pregnancies. "We help if the pregnancy is in its early months," says a doctor at a large private hospital, in response to a researcher pretending to seek a termination. "The rates may vary depending on the case, but spare between 20,000 and 50,000 shillings [between US$39 and US$99]." This kind of money is enough to make a major purchase such as a sewing machine, so it is not easy for the majority of woman to raise it. Those who cannot, end up in the hands of quacks and traditional practitioners, who earn their daily bread in the city performing illegal abortions. "I paid 5,000 shillings [US$10] for the herbs I was given," says a 20-year-old girl. Even this sum is equivalent to the minimum monthly wage.

Divided over reform

"Denying women access to safe abortion is a violation of women's human rights," says Fatma Alloo, chairperson of the Tanzania Media Women's Association (TAMWA). "We in TAMWA strongly feel that no government has the right to impose abortion laws which oppress and punish women. To protect their health and rights, women must get access to safe abortion services."

Women's groups call for liberalisation of the abortion law so that abortion becomes legal for social and economic reasons or upon request in the early weeks of the pregnancy. Zakia Meghji, Deputy Minister for Health and the only woman on the Central Committee of the ruling party, Chama Cha Mapinduzi (CCM), points out that prohibition does not lead to fewer abortions. "A large number of women in this country die due to unsafe abortion and many others suffer physical injury to the reproductive system and, worse still, some contract HIV—the virus which causes AIDS—from contaminated equipment used by back-street abortion practitioners.... It is high time women were given a mandate over their bodies by legalising abortion. I believe [this] would allow women to have the service without fear and hence reduce the number of women who die of unsafe abortions." The minister adds, however, that "Much needs to be done to improve our public hospital equipment and services before legalising it."

The medical profession, including gynaecologists, is divided over the question of liberalising the abortion law. Those in favour argue that it will reduce human suffering, especially for the poorest and most vulnerable. "We doctors offer abortion services behind closed doors. People need it. It is an open secret. I believe the risks of abortion could be reduced if laws were not after us and after women," says one doctor anonymously. A similar view is held by a gynaecologist who works part-time at a private hospital in Dar es Salaam: "Most of the physical injuries could be avoided if abortions were performed without fear of violation or restrictions upon both the abortion experts and the women who need abortion."

Dr Kairuki, managing director of Mission Mikocheni Hospital in the capital, explains his views: "As a good Christian, 'no' to legalisation of abortion, but as an experienced doctor, 'yes'." Apart from the medical grounds for legalising abortion, he also feels it is in line with women's human rights.

Disputed costs

Some argue that liberalising the law is justifiable on economic grounds alone. "Costs involved in treating abortion complications could be reduced if the abortions were performed in hospitals by specialists and without fear of restrictions," says one (anonymous) gynaecologist at Muhimbili Hospital.

One study has estimated that it costs on average 1,500 shillings (US$3) a day to treat each case of complications from induced abortion. The annual per capita budget of the Ministry of Health at the time was 210 shillings (40 US cents). Treating abortion complications places enormous financial burdens on health systems in developing countries—consuming as much as 50% of hospital budgets in some [5].

But doctors who oppose a change in the law, such as Dr Siriel Massawe, a gynaecologist at Muhimbili Hospital and chairperson of the Medical Women's Association of Tanzania (MEWATA), argue that providing abortion services would be too expensive, not only financially, but also "morally, spiritually and otherwise". Attorney General Damian Lubuva says the government has no plans to legalise abortion in the near future and he has no intention of proposing that it should. "The law as it is adequately covers genuine cases which endanger the life of a women," he insists. "If we do so we will be opening the floodgates to individuals and practitioners, which our system cannot cater for. It will be a catastrophe."

According to Dr Fatma Mrisho, director of Preventive Services at the Ministry of Health, legalisation of abortion "will not help" because in Zambia and India, where abortion law has been liberalised, cases of induced abortions have not declined. Research in these countries reveals that, in practice, legal abortion is unavailable to most women [6]: hence the persistence of unsafe practices.

Unless health care systems can match liberal abortion laws with administrative and structural support, women may still be denied safe terminations.

Doubts and fears

Both Muslim and Christian leaders strongly urge people to abide by religious rules concerning sex and sexuality. "Abortion is condemned in the Catholic Church," states Archbishop Policarp Pengo of Dar es Salaam archdiocese.

Public opinion spans all the arguments. "Legalisation of abortion could serve some [women with] unwanted pregnancies," says one married woman, expressing a common feeling. But many people are concerned about liberalising the law without developing the services to support it, and others worry particularly about the implications for young women.

Some fear that sex education and legal abortion will encourage teenagers to have sex, a view mirrored in official circles. In 1992, the Zanzibar Minister of Education was quoted in newspapers as saying that with the introduction into schools of Family Life Education, modern methods of birth control should not be introduced "to such an extent that students could be tempted to indulge in illicit sex without fear [7]".

Others are concerned that some men may use more liberal laws to persuade schoolgirls to have sex with them, saying: "Don't worry about getting pregnant, you can always have an abortion...." They argue that the state of the country's economy and the low social status of women makes poor women and girls particularly vulnerable. In their view, society should not condone the behaviour of these older men, and sex education should be included in the school curriculum at all levels. Parents should try to ensure that wherever possible girls have enough money for their daily needs so they are not tempted to grant sexual favours in return for food or small gifts of money; mothers should cultivate the habit of talking openly to their daughters about sexuality and other issues concerning their health, they say.

Out of the dark?

Those who favour liberalisation of the law and those who oppose it are united in the belief that, as far as it is possible, prevention is better than cure. "Whether done by a quack in a street corner, or by a qualified doctor in the operation theatre, abortion is always a risky undertaking. We should do all we can to prevent unwanted pregnancies," Professor Kaisi says. There is a need for the Tanzania Family Planning Programme to ensure that all women of childbearing age, including school girls, have access to contraception information and services. The public needs to be educated that family planning services are a basic human right, and the media and teachers have an advocacy role to play here.

Hospital records show that an estimated 12-20% of maternal deaths in the country result from induced abortion, says leading gynaecologist Professor Kaisi. But although unsafely induced abortion is the greatest single cause of maternal deaths, it is also the most avoidable. Abortions do not kill women—or cause infertility or permanent injury—if they are carried out properly [8].

"By maintaining the current restrictive laws, we are actually denying a substantial number of poor women in our society access to the safe services that modern science and technology make possible," argue a team of Tanzanian researchers [9].

The media has an important part to play in increasing government and public awareness of the extent of unsafe abortion practices and its consequences, particularly for poor women and schoolgirls. A debate on the question of legalisation is urgently needed. As Professor Kaisi says, it is high time to "break the silence".

Unwelcome Daughters

Son preference and abortion in South Korea

By Hye-Jin Han

Thirty-three-year-old Mrs Kim lives in Seoul, the capital of South Korea. Married to a man who is an eldest son, she suffered from depression after the birth of her first child—her husband's family having shown their disapproval that the baby was a girl. Four years later, wanting to have another child but terrified that it might be another girl, Mrs Kim went to a hospital recommended by her sister-in-law as being renowned for delivering boys. Her doctor confirmed her ovulation date and gave her a suppository 12 days after her period started. She was advised to have intercourse on that day and again two days later; her husband was told to drink strong coffee on designated days.

Mrs Kim followed this regime for 12 months, but without conceiving. Ironically, it was after she finally abandoned the treatment that she became pregnant. Despite knowing that a hospital in Inch'ŏn near Seoul could identify the sex of the foetus, using an amniotic fluid test, she declined to have the test. Nevertheless, she was extremely uneasy that she might give birth to a second daughter and face a third pregnancy.

Fortunately, Mrs Kim had a boy. Her mother-in-law, who had treated her coldly until then, relented. The warm reception her son received—in contrast to the indifference meted out to her first child—caused Mrs Kim to say her only wish was to see her unwelcome daughter "live beautifully".

The experience of Mrs Kim, a college-educated woman, is not uncommon. Across all social classes, many Korean women undergo intense social and family pressure to deliver boys. South Korea has, with China, the highest male/female birth ratio in the world—113.6 males per 100 females according to 1988 figures [1]—and the misuse of modern technologies such as amniocentesis and ultrasound screening to identify the sex of the foetus, coupled with the availability of abortion, is perpetuating Korea's historical preference for sons.

The penalties for failing to produce sons can be severe, driving some women to desperate measures. In July 1990, a woman of 30 killed her second daughter, who was just a few months old. In the police interrogation room she confessed to the act, saying that she had been driven to it by her husband's harsh treatment of her for not giving birth to a boy.

"All my friends have a son"

A state family planning programme was introduced by the South Korean government in 1961, but nearly a decade later some experts were predicting that son preference would prevent fertility decline [2]. However, during the last 20 years, South Korea has undergone a drastic decline in family size. In 1966, the total fertility rate—the average number of children born to a woman in the course of her life—was 5.1; by 1988, the figure had dropped to 1.6. This represents a 69% decline which, according to sociologist Kyung-Sup Chang, surpasses even that of China "with its stringent population policy [of one-child families] [3]."

Traditionally, Koreans valued large families. But the legacy of the social and political disorder endured under Japanese and subsequently US occupation in the 1940s, and economic hardships experienced during the Korean civil war in the 1950s, forced a change in attitudes; many families began to reduce the number of children to ease their economic burden.

Unlike in India—another country where son preference and selective abortion is also prevalent—in South Korea the desire for sons seems to be satisfied by having one boy only. This may be due in part to South Korea's high rate of urbanisation—causing a chronic housing shortage and skyrocketing rents and house prices—as well as to a widespread adoption of modern lifestyles, and high consumer expectations. Raising children is thus very costly, and small families have become the norm.

Rather than continuing to have children until a son is born, couples may seek to guarantee at least one son among the few children they have. While, with a first pregnancy, they are less likely to use technology to determine the sex of the foetus—and to terminate the pregnancy if the foetus is female—couples are more inclined to resort to such measures with subsequent pregnancies.

Birth ratios bear this out. Between 1985 and 1987, for third births the sex ratio was more than 130 males to 100 females; for fourth births it exceeded 150 to 100, and the estimate for 1988 is 199 to 100 [4]. These figures "almost certainly reflect selective terminations of pregnancies after identification of fetal sex, made possible by technological innovation", according to researchers John Ross and David Smith [5].

Surveys indicate a continuing preference for sons. In a 1981 study, carried out by Professor Hong-Tak Lee of Hankuk University, interviewees were asked: "If you have three children, how many of them must be male?" Forty-one percent responded that they wanted all sons.

Nearly 10 years later a survey by the Korea Institute for Health and Social Affairs found that 61% of husbands stated they could not do without sons. The same survey revealed that 40.5% of housewives felt a son was "absolutely needed"; 71.2% said it was "better" to have a son; and only 28% said it was "all right" not to have a son [6].

The Yangs live on Cheju Island, famous for women divers—who hold considerable economic power. But the couple's views on family size and family planning methods reflect those of much of their generation. Mr Yang, 32, says: "If the first child had been a boy, we might have stopped childbearing. This is the last chance for us to have a son, so we will do our best to make sure the second is a boy. If we learn it is a girl early in pregnancy, we may get her miscarried," he stated. Yang doubted that an abortion would physically harm his wife, "for she is very healthy. All my friends have a son. I also want to have a son. If my wife gives birth to another girl this time, people will not welcome it."

Yang's wife, aged 27, wants to satisfy her husband's wishes. A few years ago, the couple consulted a fortune-teller who told them their relationship would be strengthened if they had a son. Mrs Yang obtained calcium pills from Japan—which she believes increase the chances of conceiving a boy—and takes 30 pills a day (which could cause her severe health problems). She is carefully reading a textbook on pregnancy and underlines key passages.

"I will feel restless till I get a boy," she says. "But it is far better than the old days when my mother gave birth to six children like a machine. Most of all, I am doing what I want, and there are many ways available to help me have a son."

36 *Private Decisions, Public Debate*

In South Korea, modern technology and an abiding preference for sons has led to one of the most skewed sex ratios at birth in the world.

No tomorrow without sons

In South Korea, family lineage is very important. Under the patrilineal system, only sons can carry on the family line; and, in a country where the veneration of ancestors is still practised, only they can carry out certain familial rituals, including being chief mourners at funerals. Mr Kim, 48, from Jeonju says: "If I had no son to inherit my family name and property, life would be meaningless....[There would be] no tomorrow." Even fathers in their twenties or thirties will joke and say: "If I die now, I won't regret it because I have a son to be the principal mourner at my funeral."

The traditional patrilineal system has been incorporated in the country's laws concerning family relations and other civil affairs. As a result, the name of a daughter, when she marries, is removed from the register of her family of origin and transferred to the register of her husband's family.

Also important is the traditional expectation that the eldest son will take his parents into his home in their old age and provide them with essential economic support—his wife becoming the principal care-giver. For this reason, many older Koreans still favour their sons, even after they are married, often giving them financial help which they deny their daughters. "I don't give any money to married daughters," says a woman from Cheju Island. "But I will buy my son a house even if I cannot eat what I like."

According to a 1984 national survey, the proportion of daughters-in-law among all the care-givers for the elderly was 93% across the country, nearly three-quarters of them fulfilling this role because their husbands were eldest sons; yet more than half of these women expressed a desire to live separately from children in their own old age [7].

By 1991, a government survey found attitudes had changed further—only 18% of individuals over the age of 15 who were questioned believed that the eldest son should be solely responsible for parents, with 46% stating that the responsibility should be shared among all daughters and sons [8]. Many middle-aged Koreans say they don't want anything more than an emotional bond with their children.

Another 1991 survey of 591 men and women over 50 found that 72.3% wanted to live separately from their children in old age; of the 15.5% who wanted to live with their children only one in 10 sought financial help from them [9].

Mr Kim, aged 48, from Andong, says: "I don't expect any help from my son. What I want is to see him succeed." Sixty-two-year-old Mrs Yang is so independent that she intends to prepare her own shroud. She also says she felt embarrassed to see her daughter's name removed from the family register after marriage. One man in his fifties, who plans to use his own money for nursing home fees in his old age, believes it is important to amend the law under which women's names are removed from the registers of their families of origin when they marry. "Son-preference can be avoided if [the] genealogy record includes women," he states confidently.

The ethics of sex testing

Amniotic fluid testing was introduced in South Korea in 1975. Its purpose—like that of ultrasound screening—is to determine possible foetal abnormalities and some genetically inherited diseases. While the test reliably identifies the embryo's sex as early as 11 weeks, it also carries a small statistical risk of provoking miscarriage.

Because amniocentesis is an expensive procedure—costing as much as 300,000-600,000 won (US$380-760), parents desperate to know the sex of the foetus are more likely to use ultrasound screening, which has been widely used since 1980. This is a safer, non-invasive procedure and costs between 15,000 and 200,000 won (US$19-253), depending on the exactness of the picture on the screen—the image is not always clear enough to reveal the sex of the child until about 16 weeks.

By 1986, the Korea Medical Association (KMA) was saying publicly that these medical investigations were being misused to distinguish the sex of foetuses. A year later, the medical services law was revised so that any doctor found to be misusing tests in this way would have his or her licence revoked. The KMA, backed by the Obstetrics and Gynaecology Association, decided to refer these doctors to their ethics committee for disciplinary punishment.

However, as of November 1993, only 10 doctors had had their licences revoked by the Ministry of Health and Social Affairs, and no one had been referred to the KMA's ethics committee. According to Soo-Man Suck, director of the medical association: "We heard that even midwives perform abortions after gender identification and investigated those cases, but it was hard to gather evidence."

Some doctors performing the test announce the result in an indirect way: if the foetus is male, they say "Congratulations!"; if it is female, they say "You need one more baby."

According to Byung-Hee Cho, professor of sociology at Kaemyung University, most doctors who perform these tests practise in private, profit-making hospitals or clinics. He argues that the high cost of investing in medical equipment leads to "over-competition among medical institutions [which] may threaten medical ethics. A case in point is distinguishing genders of foetuses [10]." He says that although some doctors will not divulge this information, most "find it hard to say no".

He comments that unethical behaviour on the part of doctors should be regulated by doctors themselves, but that lack of unity in the profession makes internal regulation "almost impossible" [11].

"I regret that I am a woman"

The use of technology for sex identification and abortion reflects the extreme social and familial pressure women face to bear sons. Rather than being a choice which a woman may need to make in order to safeguard her physical or mental wellbeing and those of existing children, abortion has been turned into a weapon against the female sex. Although the Mother and Baby Health Law of 1973 makes abortion illegal except where there is a threat to the mother's life or health, or in cases of foetal abnormality, rape or incest, abortion is in fact widely available and used mostly for unwanted pregnancies.

Thirty-year-old Mrs Soe, who has a boy and a girl, says: "If the second child had been a girl, I would have had her aborted.... However, I saw so many people undergo it that I wouldn't feel guilty. It may be far better for an unwelcome baby to go to heaven."

Mrs Park, aged 32, has a daughter and was expecting a second child. Late in her pregnancy, her mother urged her to have an ultrasound test and when it showed another girl, persuaded her to have an abortion. The operation caused her considerable pain, which she thought she "deserved". She became pregnant again, did not have a test—and gave birth to another girl. Her mother continues to pester her, saying: "You will surely regret it later. Have just one more child."

Mrs Jung, 28, also terminated her second pregnancy after a test showed a female foetus. "It cost me 1.5 million won [US$1,900] to have a test in a big city, and 3,000 won [US$380] to have an abortion. I regret that I am a woman, when I think of all the sacrifice I made, physically as well as financially."

A 1990 survey on abortion practices and attitudes towards abortion, conducted among 1,200 men and women in Seoul, found that a quarter of the married women questioned who had undergone an abortion said they felt "regret" [12].

However, another survey, conducted a year earlier by Sun-Young Im, adds a much needed depth to considering how women experience abortion [13]. Some women gave practical reasons for choosing abortion and felt relieved: "It is a more responsible choice if you have no confidence to bring them up excellently"; "Sense of guilt never came to my mind. It was the best choice I could make"; "After the abortion I felt reassured". But some revealed their fears and indicated that their husbands' attitudes determined their own choice—or lack of choice: "My heart was beating hard on the way to the hospital. It kept pounding until I got anaesthetised. I was afraid I should lose my consciousness for ever"; "I resent my husband for making me have [an] abortion. I get furious when I think I sacrificed myself. But eventually I accepted the ordeal which other women also experience."

No private choice

Overall, Sun-Young Im's research suggested that men's attitudes toward contraception, virility and women's sexuality contribute to unwanted pregnancy and abortion. She says, "Women...put more emphasis on contraception. But husbands' uncooperative attitudes make it impossible to control pregnancy.... Women who emphasise contraception too much are not considered decent because they are assertive in sex. These factors keep the vicious circle of unwanted pregnancy followed by abortion turning [14]."

Nonetheless, the use of contraceptives among married couples has increased from 25% in 1971 to 77% in 1988, with the greatest increase among the young and educated [15]. Now the trend is for couples to have their one or two children quickly after marriage and to arrange for one partner to be sterilised. In 1988, nearly half of all couples with two children chose sterilisation—in 37% of couples the woman was sterilised and in 11% the man [16].

Since the 1960s, the government has been encouraging smaller families. It has also tried to promote a change in attitude towards the sex of children. In the 1970s, it employed the slogan: "Let us raise just two children, regardless of their sex, in a proper way"; and in the 1980s: "A girl educated well is better than ten sons".

But in the face of pressure from husbands, relatives and society to bear a son, the option to make a private choice about contraception and family size is denied many South Korean women. Says Young-Hee Na, director of the Progressive Korea Women's Movement Association: "The right to choose belongs to the woman herself." But many women who are struggling to have a son tend to regard themselves as helpless. Mrs Kim, 31, has had two daughters by caesarean section. "My husband says it is up to me whether we have one more child.... But I am afraid," she says, because she is worried about the risks of a third caesarean. "My husband knows I might risk my own life if I undergo the third caesarean section. I resent him for saying I am the one who should make a decision."

A housewife, Mrs Lee, who had two daughters by caesarean section, wanted to have a tubal ligation. But her doctor repeatedly asked her: "Do you really not mind having no son? Won't you regret it after the operation?" Although she and her husband had agreed before the birth of their second child that they would not have a third—regardless of the sex of the second—the experienced doctor's insistence changed their decision. Mrs Lee eventually had a son at the age of 40.

Women who cannot deliver sons are pitied and blamed. Few people realise that, in any case, it is the husband's sperm which determines the sex of a child. A woman with two sons and a daughter says, "One of my relatives, who has no son, stopped childbearing. I am worried for her, but I remain silent because there is a limit to what I can do for her. I try my best not to talk about my son in front of people without one because they become very irritable."

According to Mrs Lee, aged 35 and the mother of a daughter: "I feel like crying when I think my daughter will suffer just as I do now. It should be stopped."

Gender imbalance and the future

What will happen if the tendency to son preference continues? Researchers already know that marriageable women will become scarcer. Men may wait longer to marry, marry much younger women and many men may remain permanently single.

Will women be well treated in a society where men outnumber women? Researchers John Ross and David Smith give a conditional "yes". "Brides being scarce, will be valued more, and that in combination with rising female status in general (if it occurs) should attenuate son preference," they have written. But they add the proviso: "These cycles occur over full generations...the short-term outlook is for persistence of the unbalanced sex ratio [17]."

The views of ordinary men and women also reflect this cautious prediction. Mr Kim of Andong, who has two sons and a daughter, says: "There is nothing to worry about because men are more prone to accidents or other risks." Besides, he says, son preference may "disappear". Another man, a father of two sons, comments: "Even these days some farmers marry women from...China. By 2010, men may be able to marry women from Brazil, Philippines and other countries."

Mrs Kim, aged 34, says: "When I meet my friends, we talk about how hard it would be for our sons to get married. But I am confident my son will find a partner, however rare women may be." But Mrs Shin (32), who had a son without any sex investigations, protests: "I hate some parents for what they have done. Why should my innocent son fall prey to their greed?"

But sex imbalance, and the potential problem of a shortage of women of marriageable age, is arguably less important than that of the serious undervaluing of women which the aborting of female foetuses implies.

For Korean women to be free to have children of either sex, the social structures which give rise to deep-rooted son preference need to be corrected. Although there have been calls for abortion reform, few voices have been raised opposing the social pressures which force women to terminate female foetuses. Professor Kyung-Sup

Chang points out that in five or 10 years' time, when the sex imbalance among young people of marriageable age becomes evident, son preference will be a matter of concern and debate. But at present the issue—if discussed at all—seems confined to academic journals, and women's health and rights campaigners have been surprisingly silent, choosing instead to focus on other inequities. Young-Hee Na says: "Now we are struggling to prevent sex-related violations and to increase women's employment. We don't have any programme related to abortion for now."

If women were valued equally within society, with employment opportunities and rights equal to those of men, female foetuses would not be aborted to satisfy tradition or prejudice.

According to Professor Chang, the adoption of a new philosophy and set of values will be required: "In Korean society, people try to find too much meaning in raising, influencing, and relying on their children, especially sons.... Stressful and unstable social relations at work [cause people to] withdraw all attachment and commitment to society and indulge in family ties. Such indulgence...is not just a pursuit of emotional relief but a desperate desire to make their children compete successfully in society. People think that only sons can live up to such desire [18]."

The changes required for women to attain equal status with men are wide-ranging and fundamental. Professor Chang also calls upon the state to show more willingness "to strictly enforce its law...against senseless parents and doctors" [19].

Fortunately, among all generations, thinking is changing. Almost half of all South Koreans now believe responsibility for caring for their parents in old age should be shared among sons and daughters. Some younger couples are less concerned about bearing sons. Mr and Mrs Park, a couple in their late twenties, hoped for a daughter and chose only girls' names. They did not use sex identification tests and were delighted when a daughter was born. They firmly believe that boys and girls are equally valuable.

Charity will not Liberate Women

Female genital mutilation in Burkina Faso

By Lucie Aimée Kéré and Isabelle Tapsoba

Awa, aged 30, has been in labour for 10 hours in a maternity ward in a suburb of Ouagadougou. Her companion, an old aunt, discreetly asks one of the midwives on duty:
"Could you do us a small favour?"
"Yes?"
"When the baby comes, could you clip it off? The `thing' doesn't seem to have been all cut off."
"What? Clip it off?"
"Yes, please."
Shocked, midwife Jeanne Akotionga shouts to her colleagues to call the police.
"This old woman wants me to excise her niece again!"
The aunt, panicking, apologises profusely, says she's ignorant, that the young woman herself wants it, and admits she's afraid for the baby's life.

An entrenched practice

Despite a dearth of statistics on the extent of genital mutilation in Burkina Faso, anecdotal information suggests up to 70% of women could be affected [1], although the practice seems to be declining.

According to Dr Michel Akotionga, gynaecologist at the National Hospital Centre in the capital, Ouagadougou, the practice most commonly performed is excision, which usually consists of clitoridectomy, or removal of the clitoris, one of the erectile organs of the female sex and a major erogenous zone. Frequently, though, it also involves the removal of the labia minora, and sometimes the labia majora. The last variation is fairly uncommon, according to Dr Akotionga, and can result from lack of dexterity or failing vision on the part of older women, who are the usual practitioners of excision. Infibulation—closing the genitals by stitching or with a clasp—is not generally practised in Burkina Faso, but extensive excision can have a similar result if the mutilated labia heal together, partially blocking the entrance to the vagina.

Although excision is geographically and ethnically widespread, it is unknown among certain groups and castes, and families of one ethnic group who excise their daughters may live close to other groups opposed to the practice.

While it crosses all social classes and backgrounds, increasing numbers of educated parents are strongly opposed to the practice. However, they are sometimes powerless in the face of intractable grandmothers or aunts. In September 1993, teacher Isabelle Ilboudo sent her daughter Vanessa and her two brothers on holiday to the family village. A grave error, since five-year-old Vanessa returned excised, thanks to "outraged" aunts.

In the past, excision was always carried out in unhygienic surroundings, with the same instrument often being used for several girls, since group excision is common. Today, although hygiene remains a problem, families and practitioners are more aware of the risks of tetanus, AIDS and extensive haemorrhaging—some even wish to see it become a routine medical procedure like male circumcision. Others completely oppose this, because it overlooks the destructive effects of excision on reproduction and sexuality, and physical and mental health.

Physical consequences

The degree of physical damage caused by excision varies according to the extent of the mutilation, the level of hygiene, the instruments used, the experience and skill of the practitioner, and the degree to which the girl flinches or resists.

Jeannette Kiba, a woman in her thirties who was excised at the age of five together with her friend Rosalie, remembers: "I was calm, too calm for the old women, who thought I was a hard-hearted witch. They hit me to make me cry. As for Rosalie, I can still hear her screams. She fought like the devil, with a strength beyond her years. In the end she was held down by at least seven women. Afterwards she bled horribly and had a wound that took months to heal. The whole thing was monstrous."

The haemorrhaging that results from excision can provoke anaemia and serious shock. Mutilation without anaesthetic, with blunt instruments, is very painful and traumatic. Poor operating conditions, unsterilised instruments and a general lack of hygiene can rapidly lead to infections, including tetanus or septicaemia, and may cause death. The girl's resistance or the practitioner's clumsiness can result in lesions in neighbouring organs (urethra or anus), leading to incontinence through fistulae (holes between the bladder or rectum and the vagina which do not heal). Excision—particularly infibulation—can also lead to severe scarring, retention of urine and menstrual blood, and long-term complications: acute and chronic pelvic and reproductive tract infections, painful periods and pain during sexual intercourse. Infertility is another devastating outcome, with profound repercussions for women in traditional societies.

Hard, inelastic scar tissue on the genitals may prevent the vaginal opening from stretching to allow the head of the infant to pass. This can prolong delivery, which can harm the mother and may cause foetal distress and potentially prejudice the child's proper development. Midwife Elise Sawadogo explains that in these cases, she has to perform episiotomies (cut the perineum—the skin between the vagina and anal openings) to allow delivery to take place. Episiotomies are extensive, says Dr Akontioga, and lacerations of the perineum are extremely common. Caesarian deliveries are also more common for excised women.

Sexual complications

Agnès Ouedraogo, 30, has problems with her husband. "I don't want sexual relations," she says. "I resign myself to them when my husband feels the need. I find the frequency of our relations too high and the activity distasteful, especially since I don't generally get anything out of it. My husband complains and thinks I am not normal." Agnes is only one of many women who finds no sexual harmony in the home. "When we argue", she says, "it is always about this."

According to Dr Akotionga, two of the main complications which can arise from excision are intense pain during intercourse and—more unusually—a narrowing of the vaginal opening which can prevent penetration. In October 1993, for instance, he had to surgically enlarge the vaginal opening of Emilie Zanga, whose marriage had not been consummated. Pain may occur because of scarring or because of dry penetration—due to a lack of vaginal secretions stimulated by sexual arousal. Frequently, excised women are unable to achieve orgasm or to derive any pleasure from sex.

"For me, sexual intercourse is painful", says Adjaratou Yonli, "and I find it difficult to get pleasure from sex. It means that my husband has to take great care not to hurt me and has to control himself all the way."

"In these cases, it is very complicated," explains her husband. "You can't let yourself go. You have to control yourself to the end. Such moments, contrary to what you might think, are not relaxing."

Husbands may also seek extra-marital affairs. Many now say they prefer sexual relations with women who are "complete", and more sexually responsive. "They participate fully in the act and live it so much you can feel it," says Charles Kaboré. "That makes it pleasurable." This is also the opinion of Francis Some, who compares women who have not been excised with "embers doused with petrol". These two men come from urban areas where it is also more common for men to refuse to subject their daughters to genital mutilation.

But the concept of pleasure varies widely between people from different social backgrounds and cultures, and from individual to individual. Some excised women say they can still experience pleasure, and report localised sensitivity in the vulva which can lead to orgasm. Madeleine Karama, for example, claims to achieve orgasm easily when the scar of her clitoris is touched, as does Agathe Barry.

Moreover, women's sexual satisfaction is widely considered dependent on, or subordinate to, men's. "Women do not have sex for pleasure," explains Dr Henriette Meilo Ngoko, a Cameroonian dermatologist and venereologist. "A woman has to satisfy her husband in bed and at the table."

Clearly, the psychological consequences of excision are numerous. The strain on sexual relations can be a powerful factor in marriage breakdowns, leading to separation or divorce and often causing women considerable distress.

Excision may also make women afraid of men, depressed, aggressive or even violent. And children can also be affected psychologically. In areas where excision is practised, unexcised girls are constantly mocked by friends who have undergone the operation. Those yet to be excised may be terrified by older girls' descriptions of what is in store for them.

Charity will not Liberate Women 47

The practice of female excision remains widespread, particularly in some rural areas.

The power of tradition

The origins of the practice of excision in Burkina Faso are difficult to trace, not least because most of the ethnic groups concerned have no form of written language. Elders quote conflicting stories, usually from "time immemorial". Some of these legends, like one told by Paul Ténogo Ouedraogo, a retired teacher in his mid-sixties, trace the practice back to a mythical Eden and say that circumcision, male and female, was God's punishment for disobedience and sexual excess.

Others relate it to Islam and the life of Mohammed—although none of Mohammed's four daughters was excised, the practice predates Islam and is not at all known in the majority of Muslim countries. In Saudi Arabia, the cradle of Islam, it is non-existent.

For many people, especially the older generation, the fact that excision is a tradition is reason enough to continue practising it. Many older, illiterate women also consider the clitoris unaesthetic—it's a "ridiculous" excrescence, a useless "cockscomb", they say, it would be shameful to "drag such a thing around".

Awa Ouedraogo, who is over 60, is astonished when told that excision is an injury to a woman's physical integrity. "I never knew that [the clitoris] could give a woman something," she says. Like many other women, she simply accepted the tradition: "This practice existed when I was born."

The clitoris is often perceived as a "male" organ which must be removed for a woman to be true to her female gender—it is believed that women must not become erect like men, explains radio journalist Blaise Sanou. The clitoris is also thought to be an impure organ, and even a malevolent one: an often-quoted belief is that if the clitoris touches the head of a baby being born, it will kill it, or that it can make men impotent or even threaten their health. Unexcised women are also said by some to bring bad luck.

These beliefs reinforce the fears of many who think that unexcised women find giving birth more difficult. Fortunately a growing number realise that the reverse is true. A 30-year-old man says: "I prefer my woman not to be excised, of course for sex but particularly so that giving birth is not difficult."

"Tame them, sober them"

In the eyes of many educated people, female genital mutilation is the consequence of a patriarchal and polygamous society which has always sought to tame and subdue women.

Djénaba Drabo, a social worker, links the origins of excision to the polygamy of ancient kings, who excised their many wives to "tame them, sober them, keep them faithful". Abbé Séraphin Rouamba, a priest at the Cathedral of the Immaculate Conception in Ouagadougou, also believes that polygamy, particularly among tribal chiefs who could have 20 wives or more, is one of the roots of the practice and probably one reason it continues today.

He recalls a case of infibulation 20 years ago, of a young woman recently married. When it proved impossible to consummate the marriage she confided in her parents. They explained that "this closure" of the vagina was done so that she would remain a virgin until her marriage and avoid the shame which an extra-marital pregnancy could bring on their family. In some traditional Muslim circles, men will not contemplate marrying unexcised women because, they say, "A woman's frivolity compromises her husband and leads to the grave."

Initiation into womanhood

In a few Burkinabé cultures, excision has a symbolic value associated with becoming adult and is carried out as an important part of the initiation rites of young women. In some parts of western Burkina Faso, the practice is particularly important and affects girls of marriageable age. In contrast to other areas where women are required to remain virgins until they marry, these women can be sexually active before marriage, and may have had children.

Excision takes place after the harvest and is followed by music and feasting. Considered "a proof of femininity", demonstrating the woman's courage to the community, the practice is so deeply rooted that men refuse to marry a woman who has not been excised.

In Péni, near Bobo-Dioulasso, a girl is excised on the marriage day itself. If she has already had a child, the operation is performed at her parents' home. Otherwise, it is done in the bush and the girl is honoured by festive ceremony. She then joins her husband to consummate the marriage.

Excising a young woman just before the marriage is intended to mark the break between her life of liberty—including sexual freedom—and her life as a wife, where she has to conform to the rules of marriage and be faithful to her spouse. One woman, who is 30, had a child before being excised for her marriage. She is well aware of the difference: "It's better with," she says. Men in these regions willingly have sexual relations with young girls who have not been excised, but will only marry excised women.

But even in "strict" regions, excision can be dissociated from initiation: girls are excised at a younger age and at the time of marriage a false excision ceremony is performed to honour the girl and her family. The initiation aspect of excision no longer exists in the central, northern and southern provinces, and is rare in the eastern province. In these areas, children are excised very young—Muslims do it on the day of baptism, when a baby is seven days old. In many regions, excision has now largely lost its symbolic meaning as an initiation, says 90-year-old Mariam Ouedraogo, explaining that women used to learn to spin cotton at this time, preparing them for the life of mother and wife.

A religious requirement?

Although the Qur'an does not recommend excision, many Muslims believe it is a religious obligation. Most surveys undertaken in

Burkina Faso show that the percentage of excised women is higher among Muslims than Christians. Some Muslims still believe that a woman who has not been excised is impure and cannot perform her ritual ablutions. Many old Muslim women, such as Mariam Ouedraogo, claim that Allah does not listen to the prayers of an unexcised woman, who is described as *kiffra* (atheist).

Sidiki Coulibaly, an Arabic teacher in Bobo-Dioulasso, says that no verse in the Koran speaks of excision. Nevertheless, some Muslims, to justify the practice, refer to a certain passage where the Prophet is said to have told some women that excision was not harmful and could be tolerated. Coulibaly insists that the passage is apocryphal. Yet, after taking part in several conferences in 1991 and 1992 on the harmful effects of excision, he received death threats, and was publicly rebuked by the head of the Muslim community in front of a "court of notables".

Traditional beliefs are also invoked by some people, who argue that a woman who has not been excised cannot be protected by her family's fetishes. This can be a powerful incentive to excise a child or woman. One social educator in Houet province quotes the case of a woman who was opposed to the practice, but was persuaded by an assembly of elders mindful of the fetishes' anger to have her daughter excised.

Social pressure

Mariam is 22 and has three children, including a six-month-old girl. Asked if she will have her baby excised, she replies: "That will depend on the old women". She is not opposed to the practice, even though she admits that she has very painful sexual relations.

Rosalie Coulibaly, a family welfare specialist in Houet region, says that social pressure from the guardians of tradition—generally the elders—is strong, and based on respect for the rules of the community. In societies where excision is the norm, unexcised women are considered inferior, and excluded from the circle of "real" women. Not surprisingly, a common response from young mothers is: "How could I not do it, since I live here?"

A journalist who prefers to remain anonymous says: "My parents are civil servants and no girl has been excised in our family. But at both primary and secondary school I always heard girls abuse those who had a *zig bila* [clitoris], the worst of calamities. I was therefore afraid and never dared say that I still had my *zig bila*. Then I wondered why I still had such a thing and whether or not my parents should have had it cut off. It was later, at university, that I realised my luck and I was not ashamed to admit that I still had it. It must be said that that was in the 1980s when the campaign against excision was the order of the day."

Unexcised women may be subjected to intense peer pressure. In Mooré in 1980, one woman, a midwife by profession, had not been excised. Her co-wife, a teacher, found out and shouted the "news" to all and sundry during an argument, calling her *poug zigri* (clitoris woman). From then on life became intolerable for the mother of three. To escape the barely-disguised comments and suppressed giggles of other women, she had herself excised.

The combined pressures of ignorance, tradition, patriarchy and social conformity are such that women, the victims of excision, are often its strongest supporters. According to Gustave Kam, president of the Bobo magistrate's court, in almost all the cases of excision brought to trial (usually when it has been the cause of death), it is mothers-in-law, grandmothers, aunts and mothers who took the initiative to have the child excised. But, as Abbé Rouamba points out, women are operating in a patriarchal society: "The attitude of men, even if inactive, contributes to the perpetuation of this practice. They are as guilty as women."

"A just and noble struggle"

Opposition to excision is not new. Early Christian missionaries tried to eradicate the practice and, from the start, the Roman Catholic church in Upper Volta threatened to excommunicate those who had their daughters excised. But the threatened sanction failed because the practice was so entrenched.

When the country became independent in 1960, the first president, Maurice Yameogo, saw the need for a continuing awareness campaign, but again this achieved little.

The struggle began in earnest in 1975, International Women's Year, when a campaign against female genital mutilation was launched with government and media support. It was strongly resisted by the population. At the time, traditions were strictly enforced, sexuality and female anatomy were taboo subjects, and excision was associated with fidelity and seen as a proof of wisdom and honour. A family who gave an uncircumcised woman in marriage risked dishonour.

This resistance forced a change of strategy. The health ministry and women's organisations decided to concentrate on raising

52   *Private Decisions, Public Debate*

Girls may be excised shortly after birth or as part of initiation into womanhood.

awareness amongst women, focusing on health issues and the need to improve the status of women.

With the revolution of 1983, the Burkinabé government officially took a stand against female genital mutilation and a number of high-profile awareness-raising activities were started. The president, Thomas Sankara, referred to the campaign as "a just and noble struggle" which aimed to emancipate women: "Charity will not liberate Voltan women, African women, women across the world. Liberation will come from their will to struggle and to understand the social contradictions which oppose women and men."

In 1985, during National Women's Week, Burkinabé women called for the abolition of excision, sweeping away the taboos on the subject. This led to a national seminar in 1988 on traditional practices affecting the health of women and children, particularly excision. Organised by the Ministry for Social Welfare, the seminar brought together people from all backgrounds from the country's 30 provinces. It formulated a number of proposals aimed at eliminating all practices harmful to women and children: amendment of the law to enshrine this aim as an underlying principle; the creation of anti-excision committees at national and provincial level; the launching of education and awareness campaigns within the primary health care system; and an appeal to religious leaders to participate in the campaign.

The National Anti-Excision Committee

A Provisional Anti-Excision Committee was set up in 1988. It produced a documentary which was shown several times on national television, and supported the making of a WHO-sponsored film, *"Ma fille ne sera pas excisée"* (My daughter will not be excised), which has since become one of the main resources of the campaign.

In 1990 a presidential decree created the National Anti-Excision Committee, a 45-member body representing government and non-government groups and including religious, political and community leaders and the wife of the head of state.

The Committee focuses on education, training resource people to run regular awareness meetings among urban and rural populations. The national media are also involved, producing monthly television or radio broadcasts, and press dossiers are issued twice a year. Posters, leaflets and teaching materials are published, and an annual special awareness campaign runs during the holiday period.

Where the practice is still widespread, provincial committees have been set up to organise activities such as seminars and training sessions. In other areas, where funds are too short to establish local committees, individual resource people are being identified and given training.

The National Committee collaborates with various other national and regional authorities as well as international organisations such as the Inter-African Committee on Traditional Practices, which was set up in 1984 to campaign against practices affecting the health of women and children. It enjoys strong government backing and has the support of UN organisations such as UNICEF, United Nations Population Fund (UNFPA) and the UN Center for Human Rights.

Collaboration with health services and education authorities is particularly important. The Association for Family Welfare (ABBEF) supports the campaign, and health workers participate in awareness meetings in schools, family planning clinics and maternity wards.

Despite a shortage of funds and logistical support, the National Committee estimated that it made contact with over 10,000 people during its first three years, but its long-term aim is to reach two-thirds of the population. In 1993 it proposed a three-year plan of action with a budget of just over 200 million CFA (US$353,000), only some of which is funded, and is appealing to donors for more support. Planned activities include making more films and other audio-visual materials, commissioning research on the extent of the practice, and continuing the awareness campaign at all levels of society.

Success and failure

The progress of education and the influence of awareness-raising campaigns means that increasing numbers of parents are breaking with tradition. "We have looked into the matter and seen the disadvantages of the practice," says one couple. "Everything is a question of education."

Another woman who has strong views on the subject says: "My mother is a midwife. I was not excised and the question does not even arise for my daughters."

While some parents opposed to the practice give in to pressure from relatives, others refuse to surrender and develop strategies to deceive "the gathering of aunts". For instance, with the complicity of a health worker, they may pretend to perform an excision but instead make a stitch on the child. Then they are left in peace.

Even the practitioners are feeling the winds of change. One woman who has been an excision practitioner since she was 18 says the tradition has been passed through her family from mother to daughter. But today her daughters refuse to follow suit—even though it can bring some financial rewards. She has never asked herself about the deeper reasons for excision: all she does is "cut". She claims that people come to her and she cannot refuse to perform the operation.

Increasing numbers of excised women are rebelling against their parents and condemning the practice. The international women's movement has helped women to recognise the importance of keeping their bodies whole and more generally to reject practices that oppress them.

But although the campaign is clearly bearing fruit, there are many pockets of resistance. Mariam Lamizana, president of the National Committee, says that where excision is entrenched people only listen out of politeness but refuse to abandon the tradition. "We excise our daughters. They can choose not to excise theirs," is a typical statement.

Kénédougou in the west of Bukina Faso is a case in point. In this region excision is a preliminary to every marriage and the practice is so deeply rooted that even educated people oppose its abolition. The challenge lies in convincing the community that marriage can be valid even without excision.

Everyone agrees that awareness campaigns are more successful in the towns than in the countryside. It is impossible to dissociate the problem of excision from more general problems of underdevelopment such as illiteracy and lack of information, including health education. The elders of rural communities are particularly resistant to change, and as they remain the guardians of tradition their opinion tends to be respected. Targeting community leaders to join the campaign may prove useful in reaching this segment of the population.

Changing laws, changing minds

Although excision is not outlawed in Burkina Faso there have been court judgments made against the practice in the context of causing "actual bodily harm"—when a child has died as a result of excision, sometimes carried out without the parents' knowledge.

However, even when a death occurs, it is not certain that a father or mother will bring an action against members of their own family. They risk becoming pariahs if a mother-in-law or grandmother are condemned for an act intended to bring "honour" to a young girl.

The National Committee has put forward proposals for the inclusion in the penal code of various penalties, ranging from fines to imprisonment, for practitioners of excision and for family members involved. These are currently under judicial review. Sanctions would undoubtedly make people reflect, but it is not certain that they are the answer. Legal experts and members of the National Committee believe that legislation is necessary, but that it must be preceded by awareness campaigns.

An uphill struggle

Those engaged in the campaign against excision know that it is impossible to dissociate the issue from the context of underdevelopment, illiteracy, and lack of health education. That is why the best strategy remains to inform and educate, not to coerce. It is important not to alienate those with power in rural areas—including husbands and fathers—and to raise awareness amongst them too.

There are hopeful signs in the struggle, as change is under way amongst the young and in the towns, and there is no lack of political will. And although there is still a long way to go, the committee remains confident as to the final, positive outcome of the campaign.

Meanwhile, for many who have been excised, the physical and psychological consequences—and the memory of trauma—remain. When Mariam Traoré sees a syringe or scalpel, she feels a deep pain in her lower abdomen and automatically associates it with her experience during excision. For her, the memory is still painful: "It is so strong that I cannot even take my children to a hospital or clinic."

The Oldest Contraceptive
The Lactational Amenorrhea Method (LAM) and reproductive rights

By Malou Mangahas

Breastfeeding is the world's oldest contraceptive; indeed, among developing countries as a whole, it still plays a more important role in spacing births than does modern contraception [1].

But only recently have researchers turned their attention to this natural—and woman-controlled—method of family planning. Lactational Amenorrhea Method (LAM) is the informed use of breastfeeding under certain conditions as a contraceptive method.

According to Dr Rebecca Infantado, officer in charge of the Health Department's family planning services in the Philippines, LAM gives women at least 98% protection from pregnancy provided three criteria are met: the mother fully or almost fully breastfeeds her child, she has not begun to menstruate again since giving birth, and the child is less than six months old. The absence of any one factor signals the need for the mother to switch to another contraceptive method.

In 1994 the Philippine government launched LAM as a time-limited family planning method. In a department circular in March, Health Secretary Juan Flavier described it as "an alternative family planning method right after delivery [and] a link to the choice of another complementary family planning method thereafter."

Its proponents say LAM is universally accessible and entails no direct cost for women. In a largely Catholic country, LAM is also a method which may help ease the tensions between the government's commitment to reducing fertility rates and the opposition of the Church to artificial contraceptives. Moreover, say some women activists, creating the conditions that allow women to adopt the method could restore to them the choice to breastfeed—which so many have lost because of discriminatory labour practices and the fashion for formula milk.

Clinical studies of LAM's efficacy confirm traditional folklore: among 422 Chilean women practising LAM—optimal breastfeeding from birth—less than one-half of 1% experienced an accidental pregnancy within six months [2].

Although LAM is available in at least 10 countries and officially promoted in another three, it remains controversial among policy makers, demographers and international organisations, according to researcher Dr Miriam Labbok. "Clearly, [among its detractors] the trend [towards accepting LAM] has been from total denial to grudging acceptance," she has written [3].

Labbok identifies an important factor in the debate: widespread scepticism concerning women's ability to change and maintain her breastfeeding habits to guarantee an interim period of infertility. One critic, Michael Bracher, has written that "the advocacy of LAM could serve to confuse women about the separate and complementary advantages of breastfeeding and contraception". In addition, he argues that it could "divert scarce resources from already inadequate health services [4]".

But supporters of LAM believe that ongoing studies will confound Bracher's two assumptions: that LAM is difficult to learn and that its use "will thwart the otherwise continuous use of a more effective, modern contraceptive [5]". When setting up LAM trials Kathy Kennedy and other researchers offered women counselling and a full range of contraceptive services. They discovered that many of the women who chose LAM had never used a contraceptive, but they wanted to breastfeed and space births. These women came in contact with family planning workers for the first time "because of, and through, LAM. We hope and expect that this rapport may result in the uptake of a consecutive method when otherwise the woman would never had used any method at all [6]".

Exposure to family planning workers can also inform women how to maximise the protective effect of breastfeeding if they are not using a modern contraceptive after six months—by breastfeeding before each supplemental feed, and maintaining night feeds [7]. The experience of greater control over fertility for women who had no access to modern contraception may subsequently lead to uptake of a modern method.

Breastfeeding: a class act

In the past, breastfeeding's benefits have been discussed solely in relation to the child—WHO recommends exclusive breastfeeding for six months to reduce the risk of infant death or ill health. But what has been overlooked are the known health advantages for women—reduced risk of breast and ovarian cancer, reduced osteoporosis (bone brittleness), improved post-partum recovery—and its contraceptive potential.

Now through government programmes Filipino women may learn about how LAM provides temporary protection from pregnancy. But as health workers and women activists alike point out, many impoverished working mothers do not even have the chance to breastfeed, let alone avail themselves of LAM's potential. From an age as young as nine, Filipino women work up to 66 hours a week at home and in the office, compared to men's 41 hours, according to one study [8].

Before she started having children in 1977, Mercy Fabros experienced predictable and regular menstruation. Now in her late thirties, she has four children aged four to 17, delivered two to six years apart. All her life, she has used no form of artificial contraception and for spells of up to two years has had no menstrual periods.

LAM worked well for Mercy, national convener of WomanHealth Philippines, a network of feminist individuals and groups. "It is easy to breastfeed if you have the support systems", she say, "and it really helps control your fertility." Middle-class and university-educated, Mercy was able to take "all my last three children...with me everywhere I went." Her work was no obstacle.

Like Mercy, Dr Sylvia Estrada Claudio, also in her thirties and a resident paediatrician at the government-run Philippine General Hospital, breastfeeds her second son. She is a member of the board of GABRIELA, a progressive national alliance of women's organisations. Her child is the envy of mothers in her expensive neighbourhood in Xavierville, Quezon City. "My care-giver tells our neighbours: look this baby is on exclusive breastfeeding only." But in order to exclusively breastfeed, Sylvia has taken a four-month maternity leave.

Most women in paid employment do not have this option. The Philippine Labor Code provides for a two-month maternity leave with full pay, but many employers will agree to this only if trade unions put pressure on them through collective bargaining.

60   *Private Decisions, Public Debate*

The Lactational Amenorrhea Method: how much information and support do women need to adopt it effectively?

Violations—which are more extreme among low-wage jobs and therefore affect women who are most dependent on their employment for survival—are not monitored by the Labor Department. In the private sector, women workers are supposed to receive 6,000 pesos (US$220) in maternity benefits from the Social Security System up to their fourth pregnancy, but in many cases employers consider this a substitute for maternity leave pay. The Code does not guarantee job security should a woman wish to add on some unpaid leave. And while the Code requires employers in the public and private sectors to allow nursing mothers at least half an hour twice a day to breastfeed, few employers honour the practice. In many cases, says Sylvia, "women factory workers just feel bad they cannot breastfeed. It compounds their sense of guilt."

Both Mercy and Sylvia regret that in urban areas "breastfeeding has a class bias". Says Sylvia, "With technical knowledge, we can fit in LAM as a form of contraception but it has come to a stage when to many Filipino women, choice is mythical. We're not in a society that is structured to allow you to breastfeed for long at all, if you're a working mother."

Rhodora Agoncillo, 28, is a layout/paste-up worker with a local newspaper. She has three children under the age of five, each of whom she breastfed exclusively while on maternity leave, for periods ranging from four to 10 weeks. She considers that as well as being beneficial to the child's health, breastfeeding is also good for the mother because it does not disturb her sleep as much as preparing bottle milk. Rhodora wanted to continue feeding her youngest child because "it is such a joy to see her grow so fast", but could not extend her maternity leave. "I felt a little guilty that I had to go back to work but I also feel bad every time my elder child pleads for a new toy and I don't have money to buy it." Instead, she wakes up at 4am to express her milk, do the laundry, clean the house and cook lunch, before going to work. Her mother-in-law looks after her children until her husband returns from work at 5pm.

A bottle-feeding culture

While 85% of Filipino mothers initiate breastfeeding, according to a survey carried out by the Department of Health's Research Institute for Tropical Medicine, only 22% breastfeed exclusively for the first month. Sixty-two percent of babies in the study received mixed breast and bottle feeding within a month. Within a year, 80% were fully bottle-fed [9].

A 1989 World Health Organization study in urban areas found worse results: one-sixth of poor urban mothers, and one-third of their well-off counterparts never tried to breastfeed at all [10]. While poorer women giving birth in urban government hospitals are more likely to be introduced to breastfeeding than wealthier women delivering in private hospitals, they are less likely to have the choice to continue for any length of time because they have less control over the conditions of their employment.

Among the poor, women in rural areas have much more freedom to breastfeed than those living in the cities. But even there, says Sylvia Claudio, breastfeeding is undermined by "folklore...that the fat child is a healthy child and one fed on formula; that some mothers cannot breastfeed because they have no milk; that one cannot breastfeed when tired, etc." According to Mila Galicia, a 24-year-old mother who breastfed her two children: "The old folks say...that you should clean your breasts with the same cloth over and over, otherwise your milk will stop flowing. They also say that when you are tired, you should throw away the first drop of milk from your breast, and only later can you feed your child." Mila also followed the helpful advice of her elders to drink "a lot of clam soup and soup from *malunggay* [a leafy vegetable rich in iron]."

Two state laws have promoted breastfeeding since 1986, but mainly for its benefits to the infant and not as a potential contraceptive method.

The Philippine Code of Marketing of Breastmilk Substitutes, Breastmilk Supplements and Related Products was signed into law by President Aquino on 20 October 1986. It derives from the International Code of Marketing of Breastmilk Substitutes and seeks to "protect and promote breastfeeding" and to inform the public about the proper use of breastmilk substitutes and supplements in order to ensure "safe and adequate nutrition for infants". It requires all media advertisements of infant formula to carry the message "Breastmilk is still best for baby", and bans advertising which idealises the use of infant formula, as well as the distribution of free samples.

An inter-agency committee composed of the secretaries of health, trade, justice and social services was created to review and set rules on the advertising of breastmilk substitutes. Imprisonment of two months to one year, and/or a fine of between 1,000 and 30,000 pesos (US$40-1,100) are penalties for violations. Seven years after the law was passed, however, the committee has almost nothing to show in terms of advertisements withdrawn or penalties imposed.

A second law, the Breastfeeding and Rooming-in Act, was signed on 30 September 1992 by President Ramos who has also pledged that by 1995, 500 government hospitals and health centres would become "baby-friendly". All would comply with the "10 steps to successful breastfeeding" recommended by UNICEF, under its "Baby-Friendly Hospital Initiative" begun in 1988. As of April 1991, the country had 1,732 hospitals—543 government-run and 1,189 private—and an undetermined number of private clinics [11]. By March 1993, UNICEF estimated that 103 of the hospitals, mostly government-run, had already become baby-friendly.

However, these initiatives touch only a very small part of the health sector. In private hospitals, nurseries are still seen as a source of lucrative income by infant-formula company representatives. Paediatricians themselves are often proponents of the use of infant formula. A fraternal culture binds medical doctors and drug company representatives in the Philippines. Doctors receive large numbers of product samples from industry, which also gives financial support to the continuing education programme of the national organisation for doctors—the Philippine Medical Association.

Zig-zagging policy

The LAM initiative comes 25 years after the Philippine National Population Program was set up by the Commission on Population (Popcom) under the late President Ferdinand Marcos. Since then the programme has been subject to frequent changes of policy, with responsibility for it being passed backwards and forwards between different government departments. Initially it focused chiefly on slowing population growth and came under fire from various quarters, particularly the Roman Catholic Church. In the programme's first decade, the annual population growth rate declined from 3.01% to 2.35%.

A reversal of policy occurred under the government of President Corazon Aquino, installed in 1986 by a "people power" revolt supported by the Church. Family planning workers were to concentrate on health information and education—minus the provision of contraceptives. Donor funds for family planning slumped. By 1992 the fall in the population growth rate had declined to approximately one-third of that achieved under Marcos [12].

When Fidel Ramos became president in July 1992, he launched a six-year programme actively promoting various methods of contraception. Today, officials such as Dr Infantado, of the Health Department, stress that the programme's philosophy has shifted to promotion of "women's health, child survival, family solidarity and responsible parenthood and individual choice". The Health Department's Family Planning Program Guidelines stress that "all medically safe, effective and legally acceptable family planning methods shall be made available at all service outlets of the department and participating agencies".

But the programme still causes controversy. According to Sylvia Claudio, "Health workers just push pills and condoms, almost without regard for the questions, the worries in the minds of the women." "Family planning targets" set for the year 1998 by the Philippine Medium-Term Development Plan are concerned with numbers: a quantifiable decline in the total fertility rate, an increase in the number of people using contraceptives and a decrease in crude birth rates.

Every year, 1.3 million Filipinos are born [13]. With 62.5 million inhabitants in 1992, the Philippines is the 14th most populous country in the world, according to Economic Planning Secretary Cielito Habito. If the current high annual population growth rate—estimated at 2.46% for 1993—continues, the population will approximately double—to 126 million—in 30 years [14]. The Popcom board notes that "The Philippine Family Planning Program has always been a strategic social development initiative intended to advance family as well as national welfare. In retrospect, however, the social service character of the program became obscured and attainment of its stated goals impeded by...vacillating political commitment and its singular focus on fertility reduction."

Women's groups in the past have often been sharply critical of the government's narrow focus on fertility reduction. "If government agrees to reproductive rights as the framework of family planning programs, if the program addresses issues of sexuality, power relations, basic health services, productivity of women, pay and maternity leave benefits for mothers and fathers, then we can support the program," says Mercy Fabros.

A question of faith?

The family planning programme has also harvested opposition from bishops of the dominant Roman Catholic Church, whose support politicians traditionally court to win elections. Up to 80% of Filipinos are Catholics.

The Catholic Church's workforce is formidable. There are about 5,000 priests, 7,500 religious sisters and brothers, and tens of thousands of lay workers; they run over 2,100 churches and as many village chapels, 2,000 educational institutions with 15,000 lay teachers and a million students, and 41 retreat houses [15].

In two recent pastoral letters read by priests from pulpits, the bishops said artificial contraceptives were "morally illicit" and "intrinsically evil" [16]. The Constitution upholds the independence of government from religious mandate, but zealous Catholic religious and lay leaders have actively interfered with government health workers dispensing family planning services.

Perla Sanchez, former vice president of the Catholic Nurses Guild of the Philippines and former executive director of the Institute of Maternal and Child Health recounted one such story: "Rosa, the midwife, complained that they were having a difficult time because 'the parish priest hounds us'." She assured the priest that her clinic promoted natural family planning. Some time later, "we scheduled one day of the week for our 'ligation sorties'. We announced this to everybody in the town. Couples came and we made sure this is what they wanted. [When] the patients were already lying down, what did we see? Nuns. They came to tell the women that sterilisation is a sin...the nuns told them 'we will pray for you'."

In this situation of conflict, LAM presents a compromise option for government and the Church. It is significant that for the first time, a circular from the Health Secretary—issued in March 1994—stresses the need to "maximise the participation of religious groups" to popularise a family planning method, notably LAM.

However, activists still stress the need to extend an entire range of choices to women. Dr Marilen Danguilan, author of *Making Choices in Good Faith: A Challenge to the Church's Teachings on Sexuality and Contraception*, stresses that "the ability to make genuine reproductive choices, to decide if and when one should give birth, if and when one should terminate involuntary and unbearable pregnancies, if and when one should even have sex...is determined—to a very great extent—by the thrust of the country's social and political policies [17]."

Limited resources, limitless needs

Four out of every 10 women of childbearing age in urban areas, and five out of every 10 in the provinces, have no access to family planning services, reveals a May 1993 survey of more than 15,000 women aged 15-49 [18]. A similar study by the World Bank places the nationwide unmet need at a higher 64.1% [19].

While most women obtain contraceptives from government facilities, some purchase them privately. Recently, however, the government imposed taxes on condoms and oral contraceptives for sale in the commercial sector, a move expected to increase market retail prices by 10-20%.

Under a system-wide decentralisation programme begun in 1991, the majority of the personnel, functions and facilities of national government have been devolved to the city and town government units. While some of these are resource-rich—being able to draw adequate budgets from local taxes—the majority are poor. Thus the poorest areas will have the weakest services.

Midwives play a pivotal role in the Philippine health care system, being involved in family planning delivery and another 17 of the 23 major service programmes of the Health Department including immunisation. The midwife handles 60-70% of medical complaints considered "trivial". But the ratio of midwives to population was only one to 5,298 in 1990. The government's recommended ratio is to have one midwife for every 3,000 people. Post-natal care covered only 45% of the population in 1987. There is no single doctor permanently assigned to a full 271 of the total 1,569 towns nationwide. As a result, there is only a limited infrastructure for the delivery of family planning.

Poor provision of family planning services, combined with the power of the Catholic Church to deter usage, is reflected in high levels of induced abortion, although this is illegal even in cases of rape and incest.

Various studies estimate that between 155,000 and 750,000 abortions—spontaneous and induced—occur annually [20]. The Health Department puts the figure at 210,000-300,000—or 14-20% of the country's 1.5 million annual pregnancies—according to Dr Infantado. Septic abortion is the third most common cause of hospitalisation, according to the Health Department's Hospital Development Plan for 1988-92. A 1988 study conducted by Dr Michael Tan of the Health Action Information Network showed that almost one-third of abortions were sought by married women aged 30 years or above, who cited economic pressures as the main reason for their need to space and limit births.

Power, pay and planning a family

The Philippine women's movement, which came into being in the 1970s and grew in strength in the 1980s, is faced with the problem of having to act on a whole set of needs almost simultaneously. According to GABRIELA, these are: "improved labour conditions, childcare support, early childhood education, women's health centres and a referral system, livelihood projects, women's crisis intervention centres for rape and incest survivors, prostituted women, street children and child labourers."

In this maze of issues, the promotion of LAM and breastfeeding among women, by women, is taking place slowly.

Women workers are pushing for compliance with existing maternity benefit regulations and longer leave with pay as one step towards improving conditions for breastfeeding. But for unions, the issue of enforcing or amending labour laws to enhance reproductive rights is ranked second or even third in importance to wage increases

The Oldest Contraceptive 67

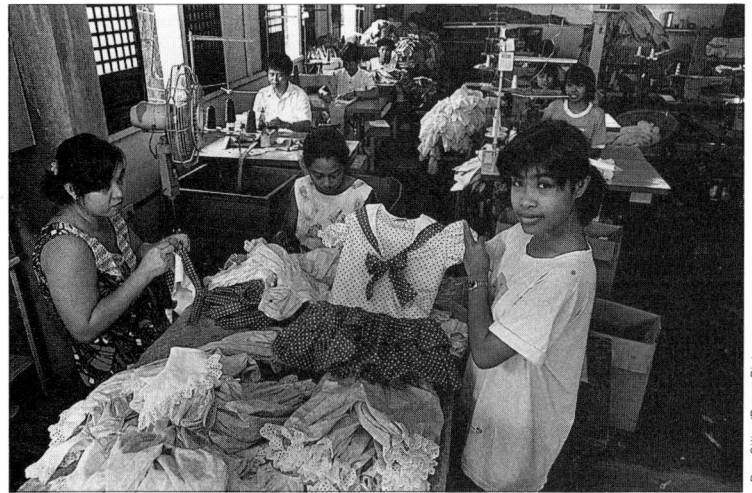

Working women cannot breastfeed without maternity rights. But this is only one of many issues that women's groups are fighting for.

and other economic concerns, equal job opportunities for men and women and equal pay for equal work.

In Cebu City in central Philippines, health officer Tomas Fernandez says the city council is working on legislation to establish "child-minding centres" in communities and offices. This was inspired by a recent study on breastfeeding and working mothers at the nearby Mactan Export Processing Zone. Cebu City is an economic boom area and the Zone is designed to lure foreign companies to locate factories in the Philippines. "The study showed that mothers are willing to breastfeed exclusively for up to two months at the longest", Fernandez says, "and then they return to work to earn some money." Even if this is not ideal, they are mentally prepared to make this compromise.

To Mercy Fabros, it is at the worksite that reforms are most needed: "A woman could breastfeed continuously if she has options on the nature of her work, on whether she could take part-time work or take-home work. She should have as many options as possible to combine her work and her desire to breastfeed." She also calls upon the government to be tougher with employers, saying that "[it] should compel companies to provide conditions to support breastfeeding." Breathing life into the breastfeeding laws, she says, "is a question of political will".

Promoting breastfeeding and LAM also requires money. The Mother/Baby-Friendly Hospital Initiative is to be funded entirely by foreign donors—notably UNICEF. In hospitals, supporting LAM and breastfeeding involves changing attitudes conditioned by market forces, says Dr Grace Ayuyao-Matriano, head of the paediatrics department at Cebu Institute of Medicine. Doctors, in particular, need to be won over, she says: "Before, we [paediatricians] were part of the promotion crew of infant formula companies." Obstetricians, too, were against breastfeeding, which was promoted only among the charity patients. Now, she says, winning the war for the right to breastfeed is the first step towards allowing women to choose LAM in the Philippines.

At the same time, Dr Sylvia Claudio stresses that women need to be able to make the choice themselves and acknowledges that, in the Philippines, breastfeeding itself can be controversial. "Some feminists say breastfeeding should be supported, others say it depends on the woman, and that the woman should have the right to say no. The former stress the health benefits of breastfeeding, and say that it is a duty. The latter complain that breastfeeding reduces women to their reproductive role."

With artificial contraceptives in limited supply, and in the context of Church prohibitions, she agrees with the Department of Health that LAM should be offered as a contraceptive method, in a "continuous contraceptive counselling process", which unfortunately does not as yet exist for the majority of Filipino women. Equally important, she believes, is that to assert women's reproductive rights—including the right to opt for LAM—women's organisations should also work to obtain "social and economic conditions under which these rights could be enjoyed".

LAM is about choice. "Breastfeeding women of the world deserve to know, and it is their right to know, that the mode they have chosen for feeding their infant has the potential for fertility regulation," states Kathy Kennedy. The job of health workers, she adds, is to assist "women in finding the contraceptive best suited to them [21]".

Choice or Authorised Crime?

An epidemic of caesareans and sterilisations in Brazil

By Eustáquio Gomes

In 1985, 36-year-old architect Sônia Beltrão had a caesarean section during the delivery of her fourth child at the Hospital Maternidade Praça XV in Rio de Janiero. While still hospitalised, she discovered that she and a number of other women had been sterilised—without their knowledge—during caesarean surgery. Although she made an official denouncement to the press, the doctor, Dionísio Cavaleiro de Andrade, was only suspended from professional practice for one month. Sônia Beltrão's case was one of many that led the National Congress to form a Congressional Commission of Inquiry—Comissão Parlamentar de Inquérito (CPI)—in 1992 to investigate the indiscriminate sterilisation of women in Brazil.

During the last two decades, the incidence of both caesarean sections and sterilisations (tubal ligations) in Brazil has risen dramatically. According to one nationwide study of women enrolled under the public health scheme, 15% of all deliveries in 1974 were caesareans, a proportion which had risen to 31% by 1980; in wealthier, urban areas such as São Paulo, rates as high as 75% have been found among private patients [1]. The country now has the highest caesarean birth rate in the world [2] and several researchers have warned that at the current rate of increase, "over two-thirds of babies will be born by caesarean section by the year 2000 [3]."

A caesarean section can be a life-saving operation for mother and baby. However, the majority of Brazilian C-sections are carried out without medical justification, despite the known risks the intervention poses to mothers—higher morbidity and mortality—

and to babies—prematurity and respiratory distress [4]. Moreover, recovery from abdominal surgery often interferes with breastfeeding.

The factors behind Brazil's dramatic increase in caesarean rates are many and complex. Inadequate obstetric training, lack of antenatal care for women and misinformation generally all play a part; and there is growing evidence that the epidemic of caesareans is directly linked to the explosive increase in female sterilisation which has taken place concurrently.

Caesareans: "modern", pain-free, profitable?

Women, their partners and doctors often share erroneous views. Many believe that a caesarean is the "modern" way of giving birth and that a normal delivery is painful, dangerous for the foetus, and likely to result in a reduction in sexual satisfaction [5].

When questioned about her reasons for opting for a C-section for her final delivery, Alícia da Silva Farias, a 28-year-old cashier, blamed pressure from her husband. He believed that a vaginal delivery caused a stretching of the vagina, which would interfere with his sexual pleasure during intercourse.

"Although there are no statistics about this, it is known that even many Brazilian doctors prefer their wives to have a C-section for the same reason as Alícia's husband," explains Shari Anne El-Dash, a doctor at the Hospital das Clínicas in São Paulo. According to experts Aníbal Faúndes and José Cecatti, this myth "has been encouraged by otherwise distinguished professors of obstetrics, who transmit this idea to their students—so much so that it has become the prevalent concept among physicians and among women themselves [6]."

The attitude of Dr El-Dash's colleague, a 24-year-old doctor, is a case in point. "My wife will have to have a caesarean, and the reason for this is basically sexual," he says unhesitatingly.

Another factor influencing Alícia's "decision" was her apprehension about enduring as much pain as she had experienced during her previous vaginal deliveries. Nearly 75% of deliveries are covered by the Social Security Medical Service (INAMPS); however, under its present, contradictory policy INAMPS will not pay for epidural analgesia—the most popular form of pain relief in Brazil—during a normal delivery, but they do pay when a caesarean section is performed [7].

Many Brazilian women have no counselling before delivery on ways of anticipating and managing pain during labour. Approximately one in four receive no ante-natal care and in rural areas and among poorly educated women, the statistic approaches one in two [8]. In many countries, psychological support before and during labour is provided by trained midwives or traditional birth attendants. However, in Brazil midwifery as a profession has all but disappeared.

Consequently, many women have a tremendous fear of a normal delivery—amounting sometimes to panic. During practical training at the Maternidade, a hospital in São Paulo where she performed more than a hundred normal deliveries for women of low socio-economic status, Dr El-Dash frequently had to deal with frightened women in labour. "As soon as they felt the pain of the first contractions, many women started to yell and implore the doctor to perform a caesarean section," she says. "They even offered to pay to have it done."

Incomplete obstetric training has meant that few doctors have experience with long or complicated vaginal deliveries. Moreover, doctors, often responsible for many patients, may schedule C-sections out of convenience. A further factor is that caesareans are more lucrative: hospitals and doctors make more money when billing INAMPS because sections mean longer hospitalisation and medicalisation than vaginal births.

Caesareans and sterilisations: hand in hand

According to Dr Ellen Hardy, of the Center for Research and Control of Maternal and Infant Diseases (CEMICAMP) in Campinas, one reason for the excessive rates of C-sections in Brazil is the fact that women want the operation in order to combine it with sterilisation. Contraceptive provision in Brazil is so poor that many women seek a permanent option. However, female sterilisation, because it has been interpreted by the Federal Council of Medicine as a violation of the penal code, is not officially recognised as a method of family planning and is not covered by the national insurance plan; a caesarean provides an opportunity for a clandestine operation. Doctors can then bill INAMPS or another health plan under the guise of the caesarean surgery [9].

Three times as many women were sterilised between 1980 and mid-1986 as during the 1970s, and by 1991, 27% of the country's married women between 15 and 44 years of age had been sterilised [10]. A 1986 national household survey revealed that nearly three-quarters of all tubal ligations were carried out at the time of childbirth, typically by caesarean [11].

If a ligation is arranged, a relationship of mutual complicity is established between the woman and the health professional involved. But the chain of pretence does not stop there: in addition to being able to claim back money from the state or a private health plan, the doctor frequently expects an under-the-table payment. Nearly 70% of women interviewed in the state of São Paulo who had undergone tubal ligation declared that they had to pay extra to have the surgery, according to researcher Maria José Duarte Osis. "Yes, I paid," admits Raimunda Fernandes da Silva, 32, a sales clerk sterilised in 1986. According to her calculations, she gave her doctor the equivalent of the "birth assistance"—a government payment of approximately US$40 made to women who have given birth.

Sterilisation: choice or abuse?

Despite its irreversibility, sterilisation is the most common method of contraception in Brazil.

For a woman who has completed her family, sterilisation may be the ideal "contraceptive", providing permanent protection from unwanted pregnancy. Until the mid-1970s, sterilisation was mainly the choice of well-educated and economically secure women. In 1971, social worker Almerinda Freire da Silva typified the Brazilian woman who consciously chose ligation—in her case when she discovered that she was pregnant with twins two years after the birth of a daughter. She and her husband had planned to have only three children. Although her husband suggested that he have a vasectomy, Almerinda made her own decision: she had a C-section and took advantage of the operation to have her tubes tied. A feminist and health educator, she has never regretted her choice and spends much of her time educating other women about the subject.

But unlike Almerinda, many Brazilian women today experience confusion, anger and sorrow because without appropriate counselling about the probable finality of sterilisation, or denied informed consent, the decision was never fully theirs. Profound regret, rather than relief, is often the outcome.

The rise in sterilisations has coincided with a significant increase in the proportion of women undergoing ligations who are poor and ill-educated: a recent study indicates that 31% of 3,000 sterilised women in the state of São Paulo had had only one to seven years of schooling, while 14% had received no formal

Choice or Authorised Crime? 73

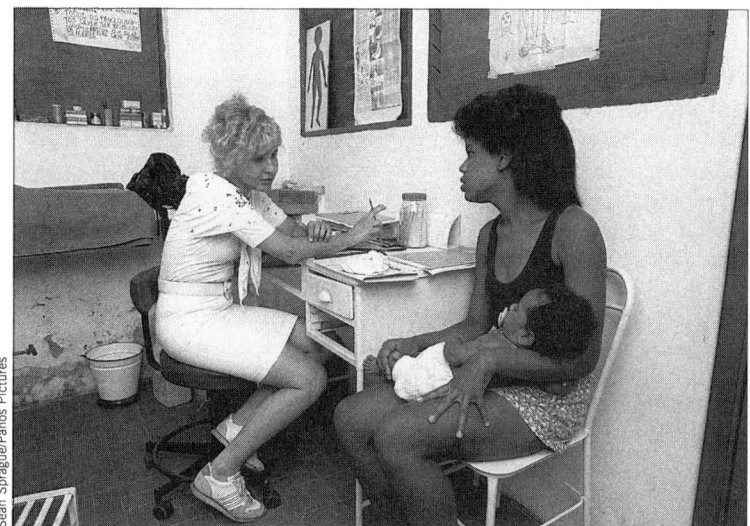

No real choice? Few Brazilian women have access to the full range of contraceptive options.

education [12]. During the 1970s, Brazil achieved rapid economic growth and large numbers of women entered the workforce. But at the same time, foreign debt spiralled and social inequities increased, a situation which continues today [13]. Many women interviewed acknowledged economic hardship as a factor influencing their decision.

Lack of contraceptive options

Such women lack the information and services which would allow them to make a genuine choice. The country's family planning services are woefully inadequate: they are largely inaccessible to the poor and offer few alternatives [14]. A 1991 survey conducted in the northern and northeastern regions by the Civil Society for Family Wellbeing in Brazil (BEMFAM) revealed that only 50% of the women interviewed had been informed by the health services about IUDs, and 76% did not know how to obtain them. In contrast, all the women knew about the Pill and sterilisation, and 80% knew how and where to obtain them.

In the case of the Pill, many women used it incorrectly. Research by the city government of Recife in 1987 found that more than 60%

of women used the contraceptive incorrectly, taking pills irregularly or more than once a day. In late 1992, the then health minister, Adib Jatene, admitted that family planning services were available in no more than 19% of national health system facilities.

A 1992 investigation among women in the city of São Paulo found that many doctors, even gynaecologists and obstetricians, present tubal ligation as the only contraceptive option for women who do not want to take the Pill, and the C-section as the natural way to have it done [15]. However, few of the women had been fully informed about the operation.

Male sterilisation, or vasectomy, is seldom suggested by doctors. During her first pregnancy, Maria Régia, then 23, suffered from pre-eclampsia—a life-threatening condition for pregnant women—and consequently delivered her first child by C-section. She was advised by the doctor that if she became pregnant again, a caesarean would probably be the only solution. Since she did not adapt well to the Pill, she spent the next year unsuccessfully trying to convince her husband to have a vasectomy: he was afraid he would become impotent after the surgery, a fear which is common among Brazilian men. Contraception thus depended on coitus interruptus and useless vaginal washes, and Maria Régia conceived again.

"Faced with the obstinancy of my husband and the risks with another pregnancy, I had only one alternative: tubal ligation," says Régia.

At the age of 29, after three difficult births, Alda was sterilised at the Hospital das Clínicas in São Paulo. The Pill did not suit her and she felt aversion to the idea of an IUD, which would be "a foreign thing inside my body". For his part, her husband refused to use a condom "because it reduced his pleasure in the sexual act," she reports. Because her marriage was unstable, and she wanted to resolve the problem of contraception permanently, she agreed to her doctor's suggestion of a tubal ligation.

Contraception has a very small place in the medical curriculum, according to gynaecologist and obstetrician Angela Maria Bacha, who was responsible for women's health programmes for the state of São Paulo for six years. Dr Bacha claims that few doctors know how to fit a diaphragm or insert an IUD. Strictly speaking, the Brazilian doctor leaves medical school better prepared to perform a tubal ligation than to recommend another contraceptive method, and better prepared to perform a C-section than to assist a normal delivery.

Without consent

Architect Sônia Beltrão's experience of being sterilised without her consent is not unusual. A doctor may decide—either alone or in consultation with a woman's husband or partner—that a tubal ligation is in order, even during the delivery itself. This was the experience of beautician Solange Dias who, only minutes before the application of anaesthesia for the birth of her second child, overheard her husband and doctors discussing the advantages of a caesarean section followed by a tubal ligation. Sterilised at the age of 20 and now divorced and remarried, Solange feels "mutilated" and longs for her lost fertility.

Besides these obvious abuses are cases where "consent" is based on mistaken notions, which no health professional has taken care to dispel; counselling is rare when there is a secret arrangement with the doctor. Many women wrongly believe that the operation is easily reversible or that the fallopian tubes "untie themselves" after several years. International norms make it clear that a woman should accept sterilisation only if she knows it is effectively irreversible. In richer countries, where the technology exists, women are seeking expensive and complicated surgical reversal.

When 19-year-old Luzía Aparecida Desordi had her second child by C-section in 1981, doctors informed her she had an infection of the fallopian tubes and treated her with antibiotics. Two months later, she was told her infection had not cleared up and that another operation was necessary. In hospital she was sterilised. Four years later, Desordi, divorced and remarried, wanted to have a third child. She was shocked to learn she could not. "I knew I had been sterilised," she recounts, "but I could not understand the relation between curing my infection and having my tubes tied. Nor was I told that the operation was irreversible."

Desordi was one of the statistically lucky few: in 1988 she enrolled in a programme of *in vitro* fertilisation at the State University of Campinas (UNICAMP), became pregnant and gave birth to a son. Apart from those seeking *in vitro* fertilisation, nearly 20 women per week who attend UNICAMP's Outpatient Clinic for Human Reproduction want surgeons to reverse their sterilisations.

Another large study discovered that many women agree to sterilisation without fully understanding the consequences [16]. In the city of Belém do Pará, for instance, 20% of sterilised women interviewed assumed that the operation was always reversible. In the United States, 70% of operations to reverse sterilisations are now successful, but limited data suggests much lower rates in developing countries [17].

One of the more disquieting facts emerging from recent studies is that nearly half of sterilisations performed are on women under 30. A significant percentage (11%) of young women interviewed during a 1992 investigation in the city of São Paulo said they regretted their decision.

An earlier study conducted by Hardy, who interviewed over 3,000 women sterilised in the state of São Paulo, found that regret over ligation is strongly associated with age, and that younger women who agreed to sterilisation lacked information about other contraceptive options [18].

At the age of 19, Aparecida Alves, a domestic worker and single mother-of-two, was advised by her doctor just before the birth of her third child to have a tubal ligation. "He said that given the uncertainty of my economic situation and my lack of a husband, I should be sterilised," she recounts. Today, at 33, Aparecida is living with a companion for whom paternity is important, but the happiness that having children together would bring to her partner and herself is denied them. "When I think that I let myself have my tubes tied, I get mad at myself," she says.

Studies have also found that post-partum sterilisation (performed after delivery or within 42 days) is more likely to lead to regret, and that regret is more likely among women sterilised during a caesarean delivery than after a vaginal delivery. "It may be more difficult for women to appreciate fully this long-term effect [irreversibility] during the stress of labour [19]."

And yet, says Dr Aníbal Faúndes, professor of obstetrics and medical researcher at the University of Campinas (UNICAMP), "the hospitals offering post-partum contraception [other than caesarean sterilisation] are an exception... as are the basic healthcare units that offer contraceptive services."

Population policy: historical twists and turns

Attitudes towards the growth or control of population have shifted over the decades. Earlier administrations openly favoured expansion, believing that a large population was necessary to the economic development and security of so large a territory as Brazil. In 1941, modern contraception and abortion were both banned. Around the same time, the Brazilian Penal Code defined as a crime any act "offending the corporal integrity or the health of another", especially when that act implied the "loss of a member, feeling or function". The definition, although vague and ambiguous, was applied to tubal ligation and vasectomy.

According to the 1950 census, the population was over 52 million, having tripled since the turn of the century. By the time of the military coup in 1964, population control was regarded as being in keeping with Brazil's strategic interests. By 1977, President-General João Figueiredo was warning Congress that "explosive human growth" would end up "devouring" economic growth. But despite this about-face, "the Brazilian government never adopted an official policy favourable to the reduction of the birth rate," says sociologist Maria Isabel Baltar da Rocha.

In Congress, positions have ranged from ambivalence to paralysis. In 1967, on the initiative of the then opposition deputy Mário Covas, an investigation of the pros and cons of "a plan for the limitation of birth in Brazil" was put in motion. However, the Vatican's 1968 encyclical *Humanae Vitae*, which categorically opposed birth control, had a strong impact in the country, which is overwhelmingly Catholic. There followed a period of political persecution which led to the closing of Congress and the abandonment of the inquiry.

The military government reflected the ideological conflicts over promoting or prohibiting birth control found in civilian society. It was not until 1979 that the distribution of contraceptives was permitted. Numerous congressional attempts to improve family planning provision since then have failed.

Unscrupulous politicians

One of the conclusions of the national 1992 CPI was that the culture of sterilisation is so deeply rooted that tubal ligation has even become a promise wielded by politicians in exchange for votes.

In her testimony, Deputy Brice Bragatto said, "There are politicians who are doctors and perform tubal ligations themselves, and there are also doctors that do them for the politicians, as an electoral favour." She told the national CPI that in her constituency of Espírito Santo, the largest number of C-sections are found in counties and hospitals influenced by politicians involved in mass sterilisation.

According to Dr Aníbal Faúndes, "the political use of tubal ligation is in reality a national phenomenon". During the national CPI, Deputy Raquel Cândido, from the state of Rondônia, accused Nobel de Moura—another Deputy and also a doctor—of using sterilisation to gain votes.

But the most highly-publicised case has been that of a doctor and town councillor in Goiânia, José Hidasi, who admits having sterilised 90 women in a small county in the state of Goiás for a payment "in proportion to their income". Hidasi, who maintained his office but had his medical licence revoked, criticises "the hypocrisy in medicine that makes sterilisation a right of the rich which is prohibited for the poor". In his campaign for election to the legislature in 1988, he declared his intentions of sterilising every woman in Goiás. One assumes that he was referring to those women wishing to have their tubes tied, but the fact is that in some Goiânian counties, the number of tubal ligations doubled during the 1988 electoral year.

Faced with financial worries, lack of appropriate contraceptive options, and pressure from employers, many women find it difficult to turn down the politicians' offers.

Employer blackmail

Many companies in Brazil claim that hiring women has become a problem since the ratification of the Constitution of 1988, as this extends maternity leave entitlement to 120 days. Women extend this by taking one month's vacation entitlement upon the birth of a child.

The knowledge that many women are desperate to work in order to support their families has led some companies to demand proof that potential female employees will not become pregnant. Women who have already had two or more children and need to work find it difficult to reject the option of sterilisation after a C-section. Deputy Denise Carvalho, who presided over the 1992 Commission of Inquiry (CPI) on sterilisation for the Legislative Assembly of the state of Goiás, heard testimony that certain employers insist on new female employees signing a letter of resignation to take effect if they become pregnant or even marry. The CPI of the state of Espírito Santo reported that four local companies involved in city transport —Viação Serrana, Transcol, Viação Grande Vitória and Docevite— had allegedly demanded certificates of tubal ligation before hiring women. In Rio de Janeiro, the Deputy Jandira Feghali accused the soft drink company Mineirinho and the ready-made clothing factory of De Millus of adopting similar policies.

The incidence of sterilisation is multiplying in chronically poverty-stricken communities, as well as those made poor by the continuing economic crisis, according to a recent study which showed that second and even third generations of families have been affected. Over half of the interviewees who had had tubal ligations were daughters or sisters of sterilised women, while 39% of non-sterilised women expressed a desire to obtain a ligation as soon as possible. Asked if they would recommend that other women have tubal ligations, 65% of the sterilised women responded that they would, citing reasons such as the financial difficulties in raising children and the effectiveness of the method. But the real indicator of women's desperation was the fact that 32% of those sterilised stated that they had become pregnant in order to have a tubal ligation during C-section surgery [20].

Elusive solutions

The 1992 CPI asserted that "surgical sterilisation of women, whether or not it is voluntary, is a subject which cannot be separated from the implementation of a policy of complete assistance for the health of women". According to the spokesperson for the Commission, Senator Carlos Patrocínio, "the abusive use of sterilisation reflects the abandonment and omission of the State in its constitutional responsibility for providing health and contraceptive methods for family planning in the context of a policy of assistance."

Such policies have been on the books since the early 1980s. Unfortunately, their most recent incarnation—the Integral Programme for Women's Health (PAISM)—was effectively sidelined during the government of President Fernando Collor (1990-1992) and has not shown any signs of life since.

In coming years, Brazil's birthrate is confidently expected to continue to fall, stabilising by the year 2050 at approximately 250 million inhabitants—equivalent to the present-day population of the United States. Not surprisingly, widespread sterilisation has been a major factor in the decline of fertility; between 1960 and 1990 the average number of times a woman gave birth fell from 6.1 to 3.3 [21]. "Whether by fair means or foul, the fact is that Brazil will never be an India," comments demographer Elza Berquó.

Many argue that the fall in fertility brings significant health and welfare benefits to women and children. Dr Aníbal Faúndes agrees—with an important proviso: "The decrease in the birth rate itself wouldn't cause the shedding of tears in a country with a population the size of Brazil," he says. "Much to the contrary, it could reflect social development—if it indicated a conscientious deliberation on the part of women."

Experts are calling for the implementation of PAISM so that a greater range of contraceptive alternatives can be offered by family planning workers in the context of women's wider health needs.

It is clear that sterilisation abuse will continue until the legality of tubal ligations is clarified, and it is regulated and paid for by INAMPS. However, Elza Berquó points out the considerable challenge of making the leap from committing daily transgressions against uninformed, vulnerable women to allowing them the exercise of conscious control of their reproductive rights. She emphasises that family planning policy "should be accompanied by policies for social development, ranging from education to health".

A proposal which would regulate voluntary sterilisation and criminalise the use of caesarean section for the sole purpose of sterilisation has been approved by one parliamentary chamber, the Camera of Deputies. Women wanting ligations will have to wait at least 60 days before surgery, during which time they must be counselled about the finality of the procedure and informed of other contraceptive alternatives.

Unfortunately, this proposal—which has yet to be approved by the Senate—will not become law in 1994, a year of general elections where even the planned revision of the Constitution has been stalled.

Although its supporters hope that its eventual passage will mark a new era in women's reproductive rights, ending a shameful period of questionable medical practices and ethics, some of those whose testimony led to the 1992 CPI are less optimistic. "Two years later, the new law which should be a result of this investigation has still not been voted and, for all practical purposes, nothing has been done," says witness Sônia Beltrão. "The abuse continues."

To See Her Smile

Midwifery, health and reproductive choice in Ghana

By Hannah Tapang

At Binaba Health Centre in the Upper East region of Ghana, among the young mothers with malnourished children, is an old woman: on her lap, a skinny baby who looks about three months but is actually 13 months old. Mma Akurugu explains: "His mother was my son's wife but she died a day after delivery....She was often sick when she was pregnant and...she bled a bit too much after we delivered her at home. But we didn't know it would turn out bad until she complained of stomach ache. She couldn't be brought here fast enough and she died shortly afterwards."

The woman's life might have been saved if she had been assisted in delivery by trained personnel or if she had been brought to the health centre earlier. The risk of untimely death is faced by almost all women in Upper East region, where 87.1% of the people live in rural areas.

The region is one of five in Ghana with above average maternal mortality rates. For supervised deliveries, 330 women die per 100,000 live births. In Ghana as a whole, 60% of the population are said to have access to modern medical care but only 37% of deliveries are attended by trained personnel—doctors, midwives and traditional birth attendants (TBAs). In the Upper East region the figure is 26%, according to Ministry of Health (MOH) estimates [1].

And since women have many children, each woman's lifetime risk of dying because of pregnancy is much higher. Shortage of services, the region's poverty, and women's lack of reproductive choice all contribute to the high levels of sickness and death.

The people of the region are mainly poor subsistence farmers who experience annual food shortages due to poor climate and soils. Most have little food during the lean season, between the months of February and May, when many days are spent with hungry stomachs.

When a family is already impoverished, a mother's death invariably brings further hardship. Orphans often end up on the streets. Two brothers aged about five and seven are new among the child beggars in Bolgatanga, the capital town of Upper East region. "After our mother died, we were not getting enough food to eat", one of them explains, "so we decided to come here and beg."

In some cases where a mother survives a difficult and protracted labour, she is left with long-term health problems. A grandmother describes how a young woman confided in her about a personal problem. "She told me she was so miserable and didn't know what to do for she had to keep changing the rags she used as sanitary pads because she couldn't control her urine. I realised she got her problem from childbirth...I couldn't tell her the truth, so I told her that it was a matter of time," she said. Like most women, this grandmother does not realise that vesico-vaginal fistula—a hole between the bladder and vagina caused by obstructed labour—is curable. But an incontinent woman with a fistula often feels too embarrassed to seek help.

In the face of problems like these, the Maternal and Child Health and Family Planning unit of the Ministry of Health set a number of national policy objectives to be achieved by the end of 1994: birth intervals to be increased to an average of three years; infant mortality to be reduced from 100 to 60 per 1,000 live births; 90% of all pregnant women to have ante-natal care; 50% of all deliveries to be attended by trained personnel; and 30% of women to use modern contraceptives on a regular basis.

No money, no good clothes, no hospital

"We have a lot of miscarriages and [cases of] post-partum haemorrhage which could be attributed to the poorly nourished and anaemic condition of the women," says Dr E K Sory, former Medical Officer of Bawku East district, one of six for the region. Agatha Ferku, a midwife at Binaba Health Centre, says: "Most [women]...are already malnourished before they get pregnant. So you can imagine what happens after four or five months."

Women who receive ante-natal care are usually given folic acid and vitamin supplements for which they pay a fee of 100-200 Cedis (10-20 US cents) according to their means. A woman could make this by selling a bundle of firewood or spend it on the shea butter to cook just one meal, but even this small amount keeps many pregnant women away from ante-natal clinics.

At Bawku Hospital, Philomena Yakong, an energetic nurse/midwife, says that if a woman is unable to pay, a kind midwife may dip into her own pocket. "But not much can be done now, because we are supposed to account for everything," she comments, referring to the new system introduced in January 1992, under which health institutions are expected to raise enough money from their services to cover the cost of drugs and other materials. Previously these were supplied by the government at subsidised prices.

Some pregnant women cannot follow the dietary advice they are given during ante-natal care because they cannot afford the foods they are told to eat: fish, groundnuts, beans and fresh vegetables. And in the northern part of Ghana a woman serves her children and husband first: if there is not enough food, she may go without, even if she is pregnant.

Most women have no income of their own, although they help the men on their farms and sell farm produce. Peter Apama from Tindonsolgo, near Bolgatanga, says men do not want to give their wives money to attend clinic because "if a woman gets to know that her husband gives money easily, she would often tell lies about going to the clinic and rather use the money to buy other things.... Nobody can satisfy a woman." His friend Apuyesi comments: "Anyway, it is not always the case that the man has money." In recent years family landholdings have become smaller and smaller as land is divided between generations and there are few paid jobs.

Some villages are 6-10 km from the nearest health post, twice the distance a woman would normally cover doing her daily chores, which also deters women from attending. But since places with health posts usually have markets, some women choose to go when the ante-natal day coincides with market day. Then they can sell something small, like wild fruits or firewood, and visit the clinic. But, says Asibi, a young pregnant woman relaxing under a baobab tree in front of her house in Kugri near Bawku, "When I get small money I prefer to use it to buy food instead of going to hospital, unless of course I feel very sick."

When labour starts most women prefer to deliver at home. "Having babies at home is an age-old practice which is still very

Time and money are scarce for many Ghanaian women: ante-natal care is more feasible if they can combine a few sales on market day with a visit to the clinic.

popular among our people," says an old man from Gogo in Bawku West district. "They don't necessarily go to hospital to deliver just because they can afford it, they go only when it is absolutely necessary, when nothing else can be done at home."

Usually, it is assumed that delivery will be easy and so it is only after the herbalist or local birth attendant has given up trying to deal with a prolonged labour, sometimes after a day or two, that frantic efforts are made to send the woman to the nearest clinic, from where she might be referred to a hospital. Even there, lack of essential supplies might further delay treatment. Many maternity wards in the region have severe shortages of items such as detergents, cotton wool, gauze and disinfectant.

Traditionally men do not stay around when a woman is in labour. And some men's attitudes and lack of money prevent timely referrals. Ayampoka, a mother in Binaba expecting her fourth child, explains: "When labour starts and we suggest being taken to hospital, the men say they have no money...[when] it gets worse...everybody runs around to help."

"Some men fear they will be asked to buy drugs they cannot afford or pay the delivery fee which could be 500 Cedis (54 US cents), half the cost of a chicken," says a midwife. But usually much more is expected of them because most poor men take their wives to hospital only when labour is complicated.

According to midwives at Bawku Hospital, there have been

several occasions where relatives of expectant mothers likely to have difficult deliveries have refused to have them admitted for close monitoring. In such cases, lack of money is always the reason and many women have lost their babies and their lives have been endangered as a result.

Poverty discourages women, too. According to a midwife at Bawku Hospital: "The women feel reluctant to come to the hospital because they are afraid of being rebuked for not attending ante-natal or being insufficiently prepared for hospital delivery, as it is required of them to take along two cakes of soap, a new razor blade, some clean rags and at least two clean cloths for the mother. These are just unfounded fears," she adds. "But if she comes here unprepared and it is not an emergency, we would advise her to go back or send a relative for the necessary material."

Nonetheless, many women are of one opinion—no money, no good clothes, no hospital. "I can't go to hospital in something like this," says Maha, a woman of about 30 spreading out vegetables in her yard for drying, pointing at her faded skirt and bare breasts.

Women also fear being questioned in hospital. "Some women will not tell us the number of deliveries they have had...because of the belief that one's children are not to be counted," says a midwife at Bawku Hospital. To divulge the number of one's children to a relative stranger can seem like tempting fate—inviting the gods to take them away. Others, who do not wish to use family planning, worry that they will be advised to stop having children if they disclose a difficult labour in the past.

In Builsa district, women have to rest indoors with their newborn babies for as long as the gods decree. To abide by this, women are expected to deliver at home. "I cannot go out with the baby," says a new mother in Waiga, despite the heat inside her home. "That is what my father-in-law says: all the women who deliver in this house are to keep their babies indoors until the right time.... My baby is 10 days old, and I have not heard anything yet. He alone knows when it will be, and at that time, someone from a different house will come and take the baby from me, then I will know."

Some beliefs—for example that prolonged or obstructed labour is a sign of infidelity—can delay the seeking of emergency care. A woman is forced to make a confession to appease the gods before she delivers. Only if this fails, is she taken to hospital. In the past, confessions of infidelity did not threaten the marriage, and the baby would still be accepted by the husband. But with social changes, including a move away from polygamy, some men would no longer accept such behaviour from their wives.

A woman of about 23 years, who insists on anonymity, believed so much in this that even though she had reached hospital, she confessed to an infidelity she had not committed. "I had been in labour for so long and the pain was just too much for me.... I thought God was punishing me because I had done 'something' behind my husband's back so I decided to confess. I didn't know the baby's head had already appeared, so I risked my marriage for nothing—for my sister-in-law was by my bed and she heard me."

The gift to deliver

Traditional birth attendants (TBAs) handle most deliveries in Ghana—about 70%. By providing them with training—to check the baby is in a good position, look for signs of anaemia and give nutritional advice to pregnant women, maintain hygienic conditions during delivery and make prompt referrals in cases of prolonged labour—the Ministry of Health hopes to reduce maternal and child morbidity and mortality. The contribution of trained TBAs helped to increase the number of deliveries attended by trained personnel from 30% in 1991 to 37% in 1992.

"I used to deliver women in this neighbourhood before the community chose me to be trained as a TBA," says Azaabgdi, a man of about 55. "We are two [men] in this community but there are others [in the region] whom God has given the gift to deliver women and we do it as well as any of your grandmothers." The skill, especially among the men, is regarded as something acquired with age.

Azaabgdi is one of 624 people, predominantly women, in the Upper East region trained by the ministry. Chosen by their communities, they received two-week courses in basic modern obstetrics. Anafo Kojo, a TBA from Nafkolgo in Bawku East district, is bringing a woman to Bawku hospital because she looks anaemic: "I'm very anxious and praying she will deliver safely.... I visit women in their homes and sometimes refer those that are severely anaemic to the hospital. I look out for *oedema* [swollen legs], pale eyes and palms, and...dizziness."

The TBAs feel there has been a remarkable improvement in their performance since they were trained. "We were given kits with soap, thread, blades, towel, brush, a plastic sheet and spirit to conduct deliveries," says Mma Alebtale. "We were taught to scrub our hands thoroughly, using the brush, then examine the woman in labour to see if the baby is in good position.... The woman then lies on the sheet propped up with a pillow, unlike previously when she used to squat on a mat. With God's grace, I have always had safe deliveries but we were told to refer to the hospital as soon as any difficulties arise."

In hospitals women lie down propped up with a pillow to deliver, a practice now taught to the TBAs who are discarding the traditional style of squatting. However, in the United Kingdom, from where Ghana must have adopted the style of lying down, the trend is now moving towards squatting—which opens the pelvis more effectively—or using other positions as an easier and safer way for a woman to deliver. Perhaps it would be better if the Ministry of Health rules out this part of the TBAs' training and lets them do what they have always done.

"What is in it for me?"

Although pleased with their training, many TBAs complain that they now incur expenses but receive no assistance from the ministry. In theory, the community is responsible for replacing a TBA's supplies after a delivery. But, says one TBA: "Everybody complains of poverty and so I sometimes use the little money I get for *kola* [a bitter-sweet nut] to buy and replace."

Many people feel buying supplies should not be solely the community's responsibility. "If the MOH has trained them, then it should support them as well" is a commonly expressed opinion.

Before their training there was no need for TBAs to buy soap, cotton, thread, blade or spirit. All they needed was their hands. No spirit was used for cleaning. The family razor, which could spread infections such as tetanus, was used to cut the cord, which wasn't tied and therefore exposed the infant to an increased risk of infection or bleeding. Each TBA also had few deliveries to do, since almost all households had their own birth attendant. Today, people have more confidence in the trained TBAs and choose them in preference to their untrained counterparts, although these still help women to deliver as there are not enough trained people.

Some TBAs are near despair. "We are sacrificing for nothing, nobody appreciates our efforts," laments one. "I leave my farm work to deliver a woman and get only thanks. I use my own money to buy everything, even the pen so my son can record the deliveries. Now that you are here, I have to leave what I'm doing to talk to you.

What is in it for me?"

Many TBAs are widows and have to fend for themselves. They are unable to work consistently on their farms because of the days spent visiting pregnant women. It is also traditional for them to care for the new-born, bathing it morning and evening until the cord shrivels. As houses are scattered, it becomes difficult for the older men and women to attend many births. Mma Akai says: "Last night I was called to deliver a woman at midnight and I had no lantern nor torchlight...it is difficult."

The lack of financial assistance to TBAs poses a threat to the programme, but the Ministry insists that the TBAs be supported by their communities. David Kpanja, a senior technical officer with the MOH Regional Training Unit says an educational programme has been drawn up to help communities understand that it is their responsibility to support the TBAs. "We think it will work this time," he says. "About 600 new TBAs will be trained in 1994 and all the old ones given refresher training," he adds.

Some midwives responsible for supporting and supervising TBAs say the training is geographically uneven, with communities near health institutions having more trained TBAs than those further away. Training and supervision of far-flung TBAs is clearly restricted by lack of transport. When midwives share transport with other programme groups such as MCH outreach services, they feel hard pressed. "By the time I visit two or three TBAs, the MCH people are ready to go and I have to leave," says a midwife at Navrongo Hospital in Kassena Nankana district.

"A channel for life"

"You know, I will say I've achieved my ambition. I had always wanted to be a midwife, to help the sick, especially the women, in their time of need. I like to support her through the pain and see her smile when the baby is presented to her," says a young newly qualified midwife who has just started work at Korle-Bu Teaching Hospital in Accra. The other young midwives agree.

But midwives—qualified nurses specialising in midwifery—face some of the same problems as TBAs. One who has been in practice for over 15 years complains: "Frustration will drive some of us away. Look at the conditions under which we work. Sometimes we don't even get common soap to wash our hands. And that is not all, I have worked so many years but never once had any refresher course or something to keep me abreast with time. We just go along with the old knowledge and depend on experience."

Edith Ocloo, principal nursing officer at the midwifery training school in Kumasi believes that midwifery in Ghana still has a long way to go: "Unless something positive is done to raise the standards...it will be very frustrating to those who genuinely wish to work diligently and be a channel for life.... It is sad to note that in the public health care programmes of this country there is no specific representation of midwifery personnel at the national, regional and district levels." If there were, it would be possible to organise courses for midwives and update their knowledge of new trends. "But in the field of midwifery", she says, "such facilities are totally non-existent."

"Things are now changing"

With adequate training, midwives and TBAs could take on a wider responsibility in the realm of general maternal care. Already they are the main dispensers of contraceptives (although these also have commercial outlets) and providers of family planning information.

While TBAs dispense only condoms and spermicides—and give basic education on family planning—midwives give in-depth counselling and dispense oral contraception, Depo Provera and IUDs as well as condoms. Dr Kwame Adogboba, director of health services for the Upper East region, outlines plans for increased family planning provision: "People will be trained, including more traditional birth attendants...to distribute family planning devices."

Although Ghana started promoting modern family planning over 20 years ago, it is clear that despite considerable knowledge about modern family planning methods, few people use them—on average just 10% of Ghanaians [2]. In Upper East region, where URA-radio has made *Adogmaake* (family planning) a household name, the figure is 6.1%. The Ghana Demographic Health Survey of 1988 showed a population growth rate of 3% [3].

The traditional desire to have many children remains strong. "My wives are past the age of childbearing," says an old man in Sinabisi in Builsa district. "But I'm happy with the number of children I have. If I die today, the older ones can support their younger brothers and sisters and that is the way it is meant to be. I have had my turn. I cannot say other men shouldn't have as many as God gives them. The family must grow. There should always be men to carry on the family name."

Awuni, a young man from Yorogo in Bongo district says: "It has

90   *Private Decisions, Public Debate*

In relatively unchanged rural societies, modern skills of midwifery should build on the traditional expertise already present.

always been my hope to have as many children as my father and elder brother, so if I get money I may marry another wife."

Large families have traditionally been seen as a source of labour, a safeguard against hardship because of high infant mortality, and a means of acquiring prestige. Today, immunisation campaigns ensure much higher rates of survival among young children, but many people remain unconvinced that a small family is a viable unit. A mother of three who does not think she will use birth control says: "The six childhood killer diseases are not the only cause of death, even older children can die."

Another woman, about 28 years old, says: "They [midwives] tell us about [family planning] when we send the children to be weighed, but I have only four children and I still would like more if

God permits, so I have never thought of going for any contraceptives." When told it is possible to have children after using contraception she says: "I thought only those who don't want any more children would go for family planning." This is a common misapprehension. Some women say they would consider family planning only after the sixth or seventh child.

Atia, a man at a *pito* (locally brewed beer) bar, says: "Every good woman should have many children, but now the lazy ones who want to be idle are listening to this family planning talk. I wouldn't allow any of my wives to do it."

"You see", says Nsoh Adongo, an ex-serviceman who insists on speaking in pidgin English, "only women who wan go round [flirt with men] do dis tin call family planning, like I marry young woman, I no go allow am do dat, a good woman be one who born plenty."

Some men are not against family planning. In Dua (Bongo district), a woman who has had nine children, two of whom died in infancy, sits with her new-born child on her lap. She says she would like to use contraceptives. "But he may not agree," she murmurs, glancing sideways as if she fears her husband may hear. Later, when asked his opinion, her husband says: "We have had enough, and I think my wife needs rest. Yes, it would be better she goes in for it."

Some women practise family planning but keep it a secret from everybody except the nurse who supports them. The main problem is usually the woman's husband, a nurse explains: "She wants to use contraceptives but does not want him to know. So we usually recommend Depo Provera [an injection that will last for three months]. But others who might not like it, due to past experience of some side effects, are given the Pill. And this is only known by client and nurse."

"If I hide it in my pots, how will he ever see it?" one woman laughs. On her lap is her youngest child, a little girl. "She is now three years old. I want to rest a bit. I will wait for another year...he will only think I'm growing old!"

The role of family planning in reducing maternal morbidity and mortality cannot be underestimated, especially as changes in traditional practices mean that women are now more likely to go on bearing children from the beginning to the end of their fertile years, with shorter spaces between births. Abstinence used to be the main birth control method available. It worked because people were attached to their cultural practices. It was forbidden, for instance, for a breastfeeding woman to have sex, otherwise the child would fall sick and die. It was also feared sex would dilute or pollute the breast milk. So a husband would only have a sexual relationship with his wife after she had weaned the child. In the case of lapses, breastfeeding itself provided some protection.

Baba Adongo, an old man smoking a pipe in the shade outside his house says, "Things are now changing. In our time...a man with two or three wives could keep himself at home when one of them was pregnant or breastfeeding. But now that cannot work...You people [literates] say it is not good to marry two or more women, even the young men cannot afford it any more, so how can he control himself for three or four years? No wonder the children are never strong."

Without access to contraceptives, many women resort to abortion. Although Ghanaian law was changed in 1985 to make some social and economic grounds for abortion legal, the changes were never made public. Most people believe it is wholly illegal. Nonetheless, abortions can be obtained privately from doctors but are prohibitively expensive for most women—costing about 10,000-20,000 Cedis (US$11-22), an amount that would pay an annual school fee for a secondary school student. In Accra, it is generally said that the price of an abortion goes up about 10,000 Cedis (US$11) per month of gestation.

The consequences of unsafe abortion—methods include drinking harmful potions, using herbal enemas and inserting concoctions in the cervix—can be very serious. Dr Yakubu of Bolgatanga hospital says: "Some of the women are brought in a very bad state, either bleeding profusely or already with an infection." For many women, their lives, fertility or good health could have been saved by access to contraceptives.

To assist a woman

Every expectant mother looks forward with joy to delivery, holding her baby in her arms and wishing the best for him or her, but it does not always turn out as she hopes. The occasion could turn out to be full of pain, fear, suffering and even cause long-lasting illness.

The most enduring obstacle to safe motherhood is straightforward poverty. Nonetheless, there are low cost interventions which could make a difference. To reduce anaemia and lessen the likelihood of haemmorhage, every pregnant woman should receive as a matter of routine, folic acid and iron tablets and chloroquine to protect against malaria—which also aggravates anaemia and can cause miscarriage. Those who cannot afford to pay are most in need. Although attempts

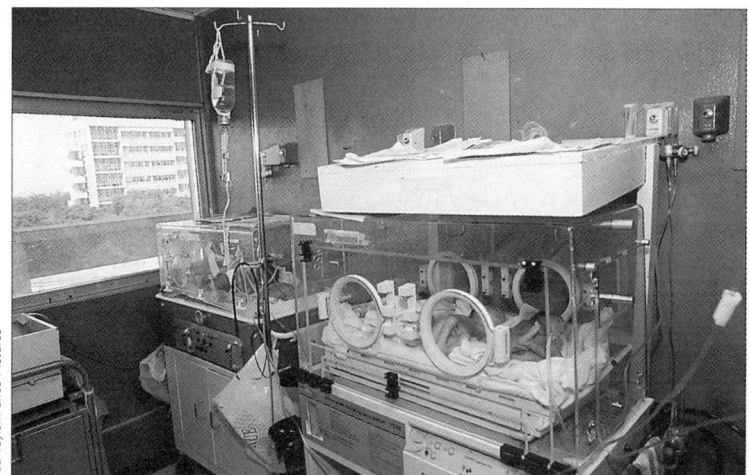

High-tech facilities for problem births, like these for premature babies, are available to only a small percentage of Ghanaian women.

to recover costs from users of health services are currently a priority among governments internationally, it must be remembered that even for the most basic services, the poorest will be excluded by fees. If the Ministry of Health could allocate a special allowance to enable women to receive the supplements and drugs they need, it would improve the health and save the lives of many women and their infants. User fees for hospital deliveries will also exclude poorer women. Service improvements such as the establishment of maternity hostels near regional and district hospitals to cater for high risk deliveries are also needed to reduce unnecessary death and illness.

For the majority of women, childbirth poses no particular health problems—and while it sometimes leads to emergencies, trained personnel can often identify at-risk women and make arrangements for more specialised care. Safe Motherhood Initiatives should capitalise on people's good feelings about childbearing and work with local practices to enable women to give birth where they want to and in supportive surroundings. The training of local birth attendants should build on local skills and try to avoid transplanting some hospital practices which could increase risks where there is no obstetric backup—such as requiring women to lie back during delivery rather than squat. More importance should be attached to the choice of personnel for training village health workers. People entertaining prospects of leaving their villages, or who are not even local, are not likely to stay for long. The TBA programme, when well organised, could have a considerable impact on increasing the quantity and quality of care for women and children, especially in the rural areas.

Just as local strengths need to be built on, so the status of the midwifery profession needs to be raised. Since Ghana is now committed to taking major initiatives to support safe motherhood, the time has come to give midwives a central role and representation at national, district and regional levels. The links between midwives and doctors could be improved by ensuring that the training of medical students includes visits to rural areas to see at first hand the work of midwives in the community.

"In spite of our problems, working as a midwife here has its happy moments—when the baby gives its first cry or when one is able to assist a woman in one way or the other to live a better life," says a midwife at the Kandiga Health Centre in Kassena Nankana district. She adds: "It is my hope that the ministry will give us more attention, solve our problems, give us better working conditions and opportunities to learn more about our work."

The Silent Shame

Obstetric fistulae in Ethiopia

By Tseganesh Gudeta

"To meet only one of these mothers is to be profoundly moved. Mourning the stillbirth of their only baby, incontinent of urine, ashamed of their offensiveness, often spurned by their husbands, homeless, unemployable except in the fields, they endure, they exist. without friends, without hope.... They bear their sorrows in silent shame. Their miseries, untreated, are utterly lonely and lifelong [1]."

These words were written nearly 20 years ago by Drs Reginald and Catherine Hamlin, founders of the Addis Ababa Fistula Hospital in 1975. The hospital was the first in the world to be dedicated to restoring the health and dignity of girls and women suffering from obstetric fistulae—holes between the bladder and/or the rectum and the vagina usually caused by prolonged, obstructed and medically unattended childbirth. Without skilled and specialist surgery, women suffering from fistulae live as outcasts, abandoned by their husbands because they cannot bear more children, uncontrollably leaking urine, faeces or both for the rest of their lives.

The condition is common in sub-Saharan Africa, stretching from Ethiopia and Somalia in the east to Nigeria in the west, and south to Zambia and Zimbabwe, where recent information suggests it is becoming less frequent. It is also reported in the Indian subcontinent—Bangladesh, India, Nepal and Pakistan [2].

According to Catherine Hamlin, the worst misery patients face is isolation. "Occasionally we get little girls who might be going blind and we say: `Let us get your eyes fixed first and then we will cure your fistula.' But they all say: `No, no, cure my fistula first, this is the worst misery. If I am blind people will talk to me. If I have a fistula, nobody will talk to me because I smell.'"

The long road to recovery

Since 1975 over 15,000 Ethiopian girls and women have made long, arduous and desperate journeys of hundreds of kilometres to the capital city—by camel or donkey, by bus, or on foot—to receive the free treatment which can liberate them from a living death. One woman spent years begging by a roadside to raise the bus fare [3]. As these journeys may take days or weeks, custom usually dictates that women must be accompanied by a male relative—husband, father or brother.

Knowing that patients may have suffered years of ostracism, Dr Hamlin believes it is crucial to provide a separate hospital or self-contained ward for fistula patients. "We opened this hospital because we feel that it is very important for them to be in a group. If they are in a general ward, the other patients despise them. They feel ashamed because of their injuries," she says. The women receive formal and informal counselling during their stay, which on average lasts three weeks but may last several months. They gain strength from talking among themselves, comforting and nursing each other and knowing they are not alone. Only when they are physiologically strong enough do they undergo surgery.

After being treated and cured, the patients are advised to return home, re-marry if they have been divorced, and get pregnant again. They are told they must have their next baby in hospital to avoid the fistula recurring and are given a card, describing the surgery they have undergone, to present to the hospital where they give birth.

If the women come without enough money to make the journey home the return fare is provided by the hospital. "It is very important that they should get back to their villages. Otherwise, they will end up as beggars on the streets of Addis Ababa," explains Dr Hamlin. "We take them to the bus station if they can't find their own way or if they speak another language." They are also given a new dress when they leave, to replace their own stained clothing.

Operations at the Fistula Hospital have a 90% success rate; where cases are unsuccessful, surgeons re-operate two or three months later. The hospital is always full, treating 800-900 patients annually. Former patients act as ambassadors all over the country, telling women in their own villages: "If you can get to Addis Ababa, you can be cured."

But some women and girls arrive with such horrific injuries that even after surgical repair, their vaginas are so scarred they will never bear more children, or they may need further surgery to reconstruct a new bladder. According to Dr Hamlin, women as badly damaged as this cannot return to their villages and "lead a normal life", defined as marriage and motherhood. Some are trained as operating room assistants and remain at the Fistula Hospital; others return to their homes to assist gynaecologists in provincial hospitals which carry out uncomplicated fistula repair.

"One of them has learned to do operations. She has become extremely skilled and has helped us enormously over the years. She is able to operate on even the most difficult fistula cases, and her success rate is almost 100%. She was a very, very badly injured patient."

"I cursed my father"

Women waiting for surgery at Addis may be as young as 13 years, with no living children, or in their forties—mothers of six, eight or even 10 children. Sefernesh was given in marriage when she was only 10. Three years later she became pregnant and returned to her mother's house to give birth. During six days of agonising labour no one sought medical assistance. On the seventh day, her husband brought the health assistant from the town's private clinic. He delivered her dead child and she developed a fistula.

She says they all expected the flowing urine to stop. As it did not she was taken to the nearest hospital which referred her to Addis. She says she does not know whether she will return to her husband's home or not. It will be her father's decision. Of one thing she is quite certain: "I don't want another baby. I only want to get cured and go away from here."

One of the greatest sufferings a woman with a fistula undergoes is rejection and isolation. In most cases she will be returned to her parents by her husband who lacks the knowledge that a surgical cure is available. But in rural households, living, sleeping and cooking are all carried out in small huts and even in her original home an incontinent woman may be unwelcome.

One woman who lost her child during labour became doubly incontinent and her husband divorced her. She went to live with her family, but after some time, was sent to live outside her village in a forest. Ironically, she could have been given medical assistance at a health centre only 17 km from her village. After two years of suffering she learnt of the existence of the health centre and sought help there. The centre referred her to the Addis Fistula Hospital and sent her there by car—a distance of 330 km. She is now cured and lives in a nearby small town where she works as a maid.

Fortunately, immediate family members—especially mothers—do usually care for abandoned daughters. However, they often maintain secrecy, allowing very few people to know about a daughter who has returned to her family with a fistula.

No one knows how many women languish alone and untreated in rural hinterlands, or even in towns close to Addis, unaware that a cure is available or with no money to seek help. Now 45 years old and awaiting an operation at the Fistula Hospital, Mulu was only 14 when she was delivered of a stillborn baby and developed both bowel and bladder incontinence. Abandoned by her husband, who remarried five months later, she remained with her mother. She also suffered permanent difficulty with walking, due to local nerve damage during her four days of labour. "Sometimes I crawled to the backyard and did some weeding. Until my parents died, relatives and friends came to see me, but after their death not many came. My sisters brought me firewood and water; I cooked for myself.

"When I reached here and saw all these very young girls, I cursed my dead father. Why hadn't he brought me earlier. I regret 28 empty years; I regret the death of my child. How I wish she was alive!"

Mulu does not want to return home, "except to show that I am human again to those people who laughed at me". Nor does she want to remarry. "When I look back, I feel as if I am reborn. I am happy now because I can see some hope. At least I can sit down properly and walk around."

After three days of labour, 16-year-old Aregash was taken to hospital—a three-hour journey on foot—where she was delivered of a dead child. "When I returned home, my urine just started to flow. I stayed with my parents; my husband did not come to see me even once," she recounts. She is now awaiting treatment at the Fistula Hospital. "We had a relative who developed a fistula who came to Addis Ababa and got cured. So, my father brought me, too. I don't want to see my husband. I just want to get cured, go back to my parent's home and assist my mother who has just given birth."

Early marriage, continuous childbirth

Technically, the major cause of obstetric fistula is lack of timely medical care. One reason for this may be ignorance about care needed during difficult deliveries. Another is the shortage and inaccessibility of medical facilities in rural areas where roads are bad and means of transport very slow.

But many other factors increase women's vulnerability. Malnutrition can cause physical stunting and a contracted pelvis as well as chronic anaemia. Early marriage leads to childbearing before physical development is completed. Inelastic tissue caused by female circumcision delays normal labour. Continuous childbearing and breastfeeding causes osteomalacia—softening of the bone—in older women and shrinks the pelvis [4]. Poverty and women's social and economic subordination underlie all these factors.

According to Dr Fekade Ayele, head of the Jimma Zone Health Office and lecturer at the Jimma Health Institute, in a recent 18-month period Jimma Hospital treated 19 fistula patients. Four were under 20 years of age, and 16 had developed the fistula while in labour with their first child. None of the women had received antenatal care. Ayele's research showed that 5% of women in the region were married between the ages of seven and 14, and 90% below the age of 18.

Like rural women in most developing countries, Ethiopian women attain status by marrying and producing many children—preferably sons. Girls marry at different ages—from the age of 13 onwards—in different regions. In the northern regions a girl as young as seven may be betrothed. She is sent to live with her future husband's family and takes instruction from her mother-in-law until the marriage is consummated at the age of 12 or 13. In urban areas

Many Ethiopian girls take on domestic tasks very young—and after puberty they are expected to marry and have children.

girls may marry later, between the ages of 16 and 20.

Whatever her age at marriage, a woman is expected to give birth within the first two years of married life—in reality often the first two years after her first menstruation. The pressure she faces to conceive is enormous. If she does not, she will be blamed for being infertile—even if the man is really the infertile partner—and her husband is likely either to divorce her or, if he is Muslim, take another wife.

For rural families, children are assets. Having many sons guarantees that a farm will be more productive. Daughters are often kept at home until they marry, assisting their mothers with gathering firewood, cooking, child care and fetching clean water—itself a task which can take up to nine hours during the dry season [5]. Household responsibilities are considered the best education a girl can have for her future life. Boys are more likely to go to school.

A women's status increases with the birth of each child. Some women close to the town know about contraceptives but consider them suitable only for divorced women or prostitutes. Modern contraception is used by just 2% of women of childbearing age [6]. A rural woman, unless she is divorced or physically incapable of childbirth, will bear children continuously until menopause; her life expectancy is only 48.1 years [7].

However, if a girl or woman suffers a fistula in attempting to fulfil society's mandate of early and continuous childbearing, she faces a harsh and uncertain future, devalued by communities in whose eyes women who cannot give birth are worthless creatures.

Men's actions are shaped by the whole society's expectations of women, and by harsh economic realities. One man who sent his wife back to her family reflects: "Of course I liked my wife. But with the situation she was in, we could not go on as husband and wife. She was not able to work or even cook for me. I had to toil the whole day with no one to take care of her or me. That's why I sent her to her family. I had to take another wife to lead my life. Sure, I felt sorry for her, but there was nothing I could do. I am poor; I can't take her to a hospital and above all, who will take care of the farming while I am gone?"

Circumcision or rejection

Female circumcision is widely practised among both Muslims and Christians. In Ethiopia and Eritrea the prevalence is estimated at 90%. Clitoridectomy is more common, except in areas bordering Sudan and Somalia, where infibulation seems to be spreading [8]. In some areas it takes place seven days after birth, in others when the girl is seven, and in a few others during teenage years.

Dr Aynalem Abraham is medical director of a health centre in Shebe, a small town 42 km from the nearest hospital at Jimma, itself 330 km from Addis Ababa. The type of circumcision carried out in the Jimma area consists of removal of both the *labia minora* and *labia majora*, causing scarred, inelastic tissue which contributes to prolonged labour—and the likelihood of a fistula.

According to Dr Abraham, wherever circumcision is well established an uncircumcised woman is believed to be *nejus* or unclean, and is shunned or mocked. She is not allowed to eat with others, fetch water or go to the market place, and no one will eat the food she prepares. No one will marry an uncircumcised girl, and anyone refusing to accept the tradition would be seen as dishonouring ancestral customs, says Dr Abraham. In these circumstances it is hardly surprising that women's rejection of the practice is extremely rare. One 14-year-old whose circumcision was overlooked and subsequently forgotten during her parent's divorce demanded the operation, fearful that she would be stigmatised and seen as unmarriageable.

There are many erroneous beliefs associated with circumcision. Mulu, whose fistula subjected her to 28 years of suffering, asks: "How can a woman have intercourse and give birth unless she is circumcised?" She also says that if a girl is uncircumcised, the operation would be performed on her wedding night (as usual without an anaesthetic) and the husband told to have intercourse immediately.

Male control

The Shebe Health Centre serves a population estimated at 250,000 and treats 200 patients on a normal day, and nearly 350 on market days. It assists women suffering from fistulae by sheltering them in a hostel within the compound until they can be taken by car to Jimma—where uncomplicated fistula repair can be done—or, if necessary, to the Addis Ababa Fistula Hospital.

Carrying and delivering a child are considered a woman's natural functions—unworthy of special medical attention. Only the husband can decide to seek medical assistance during his wife's pregnancy or labour—and he may leave this very late, or fail to take any action. "Sometimes a very sick woman may come to our health centre. And we tell her that unless she goes to a bigger hospital, she will die," Dr

Abraham says, adding that even after such an urgent warning, if her husband refuses to take her to hospital, she will return home with him.

A husband has to agree to pay for transportation to hospital. He also has to accompany his wife, or designate a male relative to travel with her.

Finnish midwife Sister Sirkku Helisten, who works at the Shebe Health Centre, believes that "we need to educate the men who are the husbands or the fathers because a woman's coming to a hospital depends wholly on their decision."

Preventable tragedy

Every concerned medical expert sadly familiar with the physical and mental suffering caused by fistulae has ideas about how to combat the problem. Universal ante-natal care, maternity villages for high risk mothers and trained birth attendants are some suggestions that have been made.

The girls and women waiting for treatment in Addis Ababa also have strong ideas. They believe that local health centres could have saved them from enduring the grief of stillbirth and the suffering caused by fistulae.

Dr Hamlin calls for all rural hospitals to be suitably equipped and all gynaecologists trained in simple fistula repair. "This will save young women from making a long and expensive journey to Addis," she says.

Sister Aster Negussie, who has worked at the Addis Ababa Fistula Hospital for the past 18 years, agrees. "If women had a health facility nearby, the incidence of fistula will decrease," she states. "And if women could be taught through churches or mosques about the importance of medical assistance, I believe we will get over this problem."

Ethiopia's Minister of Health, Dr Adanetch Kidane Mariam, has stressed the need to develop rural health services to reduce the incidence of fistulae. "We want to strengthen our clinics rather than open another hospital." She also stresses the importance of first-time pregnant women being examined by trained TBAs "who, even if they cannot screen out high risk mothers, could at least advise women to attend clinics." Nevertheless, she acknowledges, "We don't foresee in the coming four or five years, even 10 years, that we are going to prevent all occurrences."

Much of Ethiopia's meagre health budget goes to providing urban

The Silent Shame 103

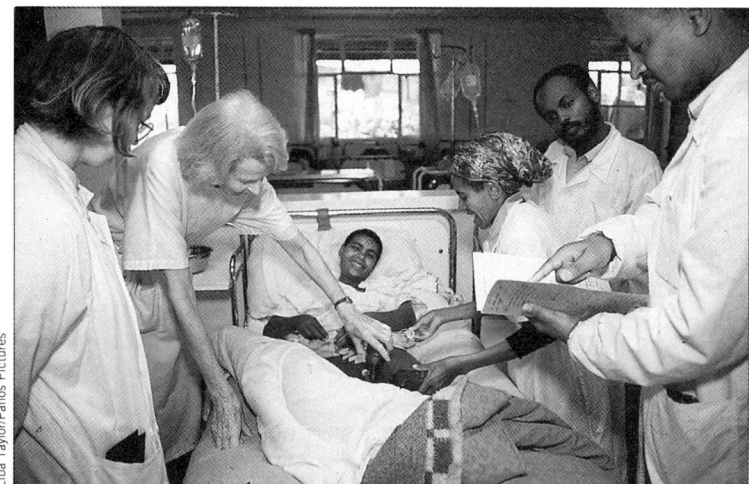

The Addis Ababa Fistula Hospital repairs ruined lives, but prevention is more than a medical issue.

health services. According to Dr Ayele in Jimma: "There is no allocation for health education. I believe priority should be given to training community health workers rather than doctors; they are very near to the people, know their needs and can do a lot to help them," he argues.

He notes that in the six years it takes to train one doctor, a thousand community health workers could be trained to improve the health status of the rural population. "But what we are now seeing is that the number of medical doctors is increasing. If we take as an example the Jimma Zone, 85% of the health budget goes to pay the salaries of the staff," he says.

The importance of training TBAs to identify high-risk women is widely acknowledged. Says Catherine Hamlin, "Fistula is a tremendously difficult problem, one that will take years to solve." However, she believes some steps could be taken immediately. More trained midwives and traditional birth attendants (TBAs) are needed to go into villages and identify women who may be at high risk for fistulae—those whose height is less than 150 cm, those under 18 or over 35 years of age, and those thought likely to have a breech presentation or multiple birth. Such women could go before delivery to maternity villages attached to hospitals where they would be tended by trained health workers during labour.

But TBAs, who are also mothers with many children, need money to survive and some are unable to take on the extra work if it is not remunerated. Sister Helisten, at the Shebe Health Centre, is well aware of this problem: "In our area we are trying to encourage TBAs to assist pregnant women. We recently gave them a refresher course and we are in the process of reaching an agreement with the government to arrange for them to receive some kind of payment," she says.

Dr Barbara Kwast, who worked for many years with the Hamlins, points out that the prediction of obstructed labour through ante-natal care has a worryingly low sensitivity. Nonetheless, Dr Kwast and UK surgeon Dr John Kelly, who is annually seconded to the Addis Fistula Hospital, both support the call for maternity waiting homes [9].

Because maternity waiting homes may only reach a proportion of at-risk women—since not all high-risk pregnancies are identified through ante-natal care, Dr Kwast believes there needs to be more research into prolonged labour, in order to increase understanding of the signals that trigger people to seek expert help and why it is often delayed. TBAs should be trained to send women who are not making progress in labour to the health centre, before the stage of obstruction and before they endure days of painful labour [10].

Changing destiny

Clearly, deeply rooted practices such as female circumcision and child marriage which contribute to the incidence of fistulae will not be changed through legislation alone. Under the 1987 Constitution the minimum age for marriage for both sexes is officially 18 years but the health minister says that in practice there is still a need "to teach the public to raise the age of marriage".

Some women recognise the strain of early marriage and continuous childbearing. But they say they are helpless and have no choice—this is what is required in order to be a "whole woman". Without information about the causes of fistulae, many women attribute their affliction to the "evil eye" or "will of God" as do their husbands.

An elderly priest who brought his wife to be cured at the Addis Ababa Fistula hospital states categorically: "No one can do anything to prevent a fistula. Early marriage is not a cause; I saw with my own eyes my wife, who was 38 years old, develop a fistula while giving birth to our eighth child. It is a destiny written by God—and does anyone have the power to change that?"

One plan under consideration is for health educators to liaise with workers from the Ministry of Agriculture—who have contact with rural farmers—so they can teach men about the importance of women's ante-natal and post-natal care.

The overriding reality in rural areas is that most people who learn about the value of medical care do so through an experience of great suffering.

A former patient at the Addis Fistula Hospital, Ade Temmam, was 40 years old when she developed a fistula while giving birth to her eighth child, delivered stillborn after three days of labour.

Fortunately, during the three months that she suffered from the fistula her family was beside her, including her husband who has a second wife. Recalling the time when she was incontinent and helpless, unable to live as a married woman, and filled with a sense of shame, she says: "I was always worried...always begging my Creator to cure me. I could not help the situation I was in.... I always felt it when my children took my clothes to wash. I was embarrassed and felt inferior."

Ade Temmam is cured now, but she says: "I can't carry heavy things like water or firewood. Now when I have sex, it is painful for me. My husband knows about it and we do it carefully. I sometimes think of abstinence, but my marriage depends on it. What kind of marriage will it be without sex? So I have to comply with my situation."

Ade was fortunate that when the Jimma hospital which did her repair recommended sterilisation her husband agreed; although women can decide themselves about the use of other types of family planning methods, sterilisation requires the husband's consent. But Ade's decision to undergo ligation was difficult. "One can never say I have enough children. I agreed to the operation because giving birth has become a risk to my life. Now my husband and I have accepted our situation and we live by it," she says.

Her husband comments: "She is my first wife. Even [though] I have two wives, after she became ill, I used to come more frequently to see her.... Looking back, I compare that time to living with a corpse. After the operation we were told to abstain from sex for six months. We respected that and now we are doing it carefully. I care for her because she is mine."

He admits that until his wife's last labour he did not understand the value of seeking medical assistance. "When someone felt sick, we used to kill goats and pray. But from teachings at the mosque and seeing somebody sick getting better after medical assistance, I changed my attitude," he explains.

"When my wife was sick, I didn't delay her going to the hospital. The doctors gave us a solution for our problem and worry. Our big problem in the area is lack of an adequate medical facility. If we have that, everything will be all right."

But until attitudes and traditions change and health care services are strengthened, the only chance for many damaged and distressed girls and women is to make the long and expensive journey in search of a cure.

Double Standard, Double Threat

HIV and reproductive health in Thailand

By Suwanna Asavaroengchai

"I was thinking of cutting him into pieces," says Kanda, trying to control her trembling voice. "He has ruined my life and our children's too."

Kanda was over four months pregnant with her second child when she tested positive for HIV. The source of her infection: her quiet husband, whom she had not suspected of having sex with other women. So she had not thought to protect herself—or her younger child, who is now three months old.

During ante-natal care in a hospital in Bangkok, Niramol was unceremoniously pronounced HIV-positive. Abortion was recommended. "But", said the health worker bluntly, "all the hospital's beds are fully occupied. You should go to another hospital." Her medical fee, which she had paid in advance, and her health documents were hastily returned to her. The shock of being turned out of the hospital made her feel, she says, like a criminal.

Explosive epidemic

Over half a million people in Thailand—nearly 1% of the population—are estimated to have HIV, and by the year 2000, the Public Health Ministry estimates that 1.6 million adults will be infected, with roughly equal numbers of men and women. Cumulatively 2.2 million people will have been infected [1]. By comparison, the United States, where the epidemic has existed for at least five years longer in a population four times that of Thailand, the estimated figure is one million [2].

Social norms encourage Thai men, married or single, to visit brothels regularly, and an illegal but hugely powerful sex industry—boosted by foreign tourism and social dislocation—is fuelling the spread of the HIV virus. And HIV flourishes through another channel. Thailand has a large drug-injecting community, being the gateway of several heroin-exporting routes.

General statistics indicate most HIV-positive people are working-class, but a recent survey conducted at five of the most expensive private hospitals in Bangkok suggests growing numbers among the Thai middle-class: 0.5% of the patients, male and female, were HIV-positive [3].

In the 10 years since AIDS first became apparent in the country, the number of women with AIDS has increased sharply and new cases among women are predicted to match those among men in the near future [4]. Of approximately 7,450 cases of AIDS and AIDS-related complex (ARC), 12.5% and 15% respectively are women. About 1% of pregnant women are HIV-positive, which translates into about 10,000 cases a year [5].

These pregnant women have an obvious dilemma, but all women wanting to conceive are threatened by the epidemic: reproductive sex is unsafe sex. Campaigns which treat HIV/AIDS primarily as a matter of sexual health and focus on changing sexual behaviour by encouraging condom use, while neglecting to tackle the social norms which condone different standards of behaviour for men, do little to increase women's power to protect themselves and their future children.

One-sided monogamy

In Thailand, men hold the leading roles in many areas, not least in the area of sexuality. Thai women of all classes have traditionally been expected to be virgins when they marry and to uphold a "one-sided monogamy" thereafter [6]. But men are free to have sex with other women, on the basis that having many partners proves a man's virility. Reports suggest that 90% of Thai males engage in commercial sex at some point in their lives [7].

A survey of 1,200 teenage students in Chiang Mai—two-thirds of them women—found the majority consider it "natural" for men to visit brothels [8]. Another survey of 444 men between the ages of 17 and 24, living in slum communities in Bangkok and the northeastern city of Udonthani, found 41% had their first intercourse with sex workers—at an average age of 16 years—and 60% said they visited brothels between one and 55 times each year [9].

Thira, in his early thirties, says conceitedly: "It's a man's personal pride to have sex with a lot of women. It proves our manhood." He and his single and married friends went drinking before visiting brothels, almost every weekend, ever since they were teenagers. Now HIV-positive, Thira has a girlfriend whom he would have married had he not been infected: "She knew well that I visited brothels. She never asked me to stop. But if she had, I wouldn't have listened anyway."

Until recently, any woman who "lost" her virginity before marriage would "depreciate in value", and if it became public knowledge that a man had "won" her virginity from her she would bring disgrace on herself and her family. But Thai society has witnessed dramatic changes and sex before marriage is now not uncommon. Even if the new social norm does not formally accept this, it does not reject it as fiercely as before.

Once married, a woman gains little in sexual status. If she has an extramarital affair she is likely to be punished with divorce, whereas men's affairs are widely tolerated. A man can have numerous sexual relationships as long as he meets the financial needs of his family. Women are reluctant to rock the boat, knowing they will receive little sympathy—from the public or from the divorce court—if a husband is considered a "responsible man". Even when husbands do not take financial responsibility, many women dare not break up the

Men's responsibilities for their families must include protecting their future children against the threat of HIV.

family because they are the ones who will be blamed.

Pranee, a housewife in Chiang Mai says, "I don't want to hear anything about AIDS as I can't do anything at all. If my working husband drops into somewhere [sex establishments], that's beyond my control. If anything [HIV infection] occurs, so be it."

Women's lack of power in their sexual relationships has devastating implications. "For married women, it has become high-risk behaviour to have unprotected sex with their husbands, unless they are absolutely certain that their husbands are not visiting sex establishments," says Jon Ungphakorn, AIDS activist and director of the AIDS counselling service Access [10].

Condom campaigns: a partial answer

In an effort to curtail the invasion of AIDS, the government launched a campaign in 1989 to promote "100% condom use" in sex establishments, since when over 60 million condoms have been distributed annually to the country's 6,029 sex establishments [11].

Since the campaign began, use of condoms has shot up from 5-6% to as high as 90% in some areas, according to Dr Prayura Kunasol, director-general of the Department of Communicable Disease Control (CDC) in the Ministry of Public Health. The messages about the dangers of HIV has also reduced the numbers of men visiting brothels. According to Dr Chavalit Mangkalaviraj, a preventive medicine expert in the CDC's Division of Venereal Diseases, the latest survey, conducted in July 1993, indicated that one prostitute has, on average, 1.8-2.7 clients a day, compared with 3.5 clients four years ago.

Another, powerful, indicator of the condom campaign's effectiveness has been the phenomenal drop in cases of sexually transmitted diseases (STDs) to almost one-fifth of their previous level—from 7.69 persons per 1,000 in 1987 to just 1.64 in 1993 [12].

The drop in STDs also results from improved treatment. Between 1991 and 1992, the Public Health Ministry established over 130 STD/AIDS clinics throughout the country for districts recorded as having over 80 prostitutes. Funds were also set aside for medical and condom supplies in these districts. CDC advises all sex workers to visit an STD clinic each week, or at least once a month, for various checks including blood tests for HIV.

However, there is concern that these tests are more for the clients' benefit and are in some ways being used against the interests of sex workers. Chantawipa Apisuk of Empower, an organisation in Bangkok working to support sex workers, explains that the Public

Health Ministry has no legal right to make STD checks mandatory since prostitution is outlawed. It has adopted a system of approaching sex establishment operators, who in turn send the sex workers for checks. In 1992 the government announced in its National AIDS Policy that no blood test should be performed without informed consent.

"There is a wide gap between national policy and actual practice," says Jon Ungphakorn. "Forced blood tests are rampant, especially in rural areas, where health officials have more freedom to practise what they think is a right, regardless of national policy." And many sex operators compel sex workers to have blood tests so that they can claim their girls are disease-free, thus attracting back clients frightened off by early AIDS campaigns. "Sex workers who have a sense of guilt instilled in them, for being in an illegal profession, have to accept whatever they are told to do..." explains Apisuk.

"The STD/AIDS control scheme, like any other communicable disease control scheme, is meant to protect people in society from contracting the disease. In this case, it protects the men, not the prostitutes," she says. "What are they going to do when they get to the last woman? Is she going to win the prize [13]?"

Unprotected sex: trickery and ignorance

But sex without condoms is still on offer. Sex workers complain about the hypocrisy among sex operators. As profit is their goal, many sex operators favour their regular clients who request non-condom sex. "They [sex operators] even sleep with us unprotected," says Sumalee, an ex-masseuse with HIV. "When we quarrelled with the clients when they did not want to use condoms, the operators would take the clients' side."

Sometimes, it is the sex workers themselves who break the rules. Since negotiations behind closed doors are commonplace, men will usually pay extra for unprotected sex. "If the man looked clean and healthy then I'd accept the offer," says Sumalee, adding that this was the case with about half her clients. She assumed that AIDS would be like other sexually transmitted diseases, often recognisable in men from physical symptoms such as discharge, whereas HIV infection is asymptomatic.

The poorer the prostitute, the less likely or able she is to insist on condom use: a 1992 survey of 100 sex workers in Klong Toey slum, the biggest in Bangkok, revealed an abysmal 9% condom use in brothels there [14].

In other instances, male clients get round the condom policy by tearing the condom or pulling it off during sexual intercourse. Damrong, a former hotel employee in Bangkok, contracted HIV during intercourse using a condom he had deliberately torn. "Once it was broken all the way through I would have complete exposure inside the woman," he explains. "Thus I enjoyed the same sexual sensation as if without any condom.... I was not going to pay for the girl and have to use a condom," he recalls, shaking his head at his past stupidity.

For many years, Damrong, single and in his late thirties, commonly visited "tea houses" (in reality brothels) in Bangkok's Chinatown. He repeatedly tricked the women. "By the time the girl realised what I did, it was too late to resist," he says triumphantly. Now living with AIDS, Damrong continues to blame prostitutes for transmitting the virus to men.

Unsurprisingly, men's drinking behaviour is closely associated with their sexual behaviour. Thira says of his weekend drink-and-sex forays that without alcohol in his veins, he would not have the courage to have sex with a strange female. Tid, an HIV-positive conscript, who led a similar lifestyle, says that when he was drunk he sometimes used a condom, sometimes not.

"More than 50% of men who visit brothels have consumed alcohol. Not only does it affect the condom campaign, it also leads to violence in brothels, particularly when sex workers refuse to lie with drunken non-condom clients," claims Dr Mangkalaviraj.

Dismissal and debt

Recently, Sumalee and 10 other women from her brothel were fired because they all tested HIV-positive. Summary dismissal of women found HIV-positive is routine; rural girls are sent home.

Sumalee was bewildered: "I could not figure out why I contracted the virus. I had been very cautious and had my blood checked every three months." Chantiwipa Apisuk explains: "After the government introduced it, quite a large number of prostitutes mistakenly believed the regular blood test was actually a measure of protection against the virus. Only when their colleagues contracted the virus, one by one, did they realise that it was not."

Some of Sumalee's friends have continued to find business. Jiab, a young rural woman who is HIV-positive, argues that her clients are safe because she insists on condom use. Although she has some savings she feels it is now even more essential to keep earning: "I have to make a lot of money, so that if I die, my mother and child won't suffer financially. Without me, they have no one to support them." Some HIV-positive women avoid STD and blood tests simply by not turning up to work on the days they are held. Those who miss the regular health check may have their income cut by their employers.

The reality is that although condom use is high in the more affluent urban sex establishments and among the better educated and more experienced prostitutes, young and inexperienced prostitutes in rural low-class brothels know very little about HIV or AIDS, STDs or condoms, and have little chance to protect themselves.

Networks established between sex operators in the northern provinces make it almost impossible to do outreach work with prostitutes. Women are regularly rotated within the network, and the sick are sent home. One reason for rotation is to maximise profits. "For example," says Apisuk, "a prostitute with a debt of 10,000 baht [US$270]—the money was paid in advance to her parents in exchange for the girl—has to work for six months to be free from debt. In the fifth month, the brothel owner resells her to another brothel in the same network at a price between 6,000-8,000 baht [US$162-216]. The same prostitute then has to begin to work off the new debt at the new brothel for another owner. After three months, the new brothel resells her for 3,000 baht [US$81] to another brothel." The exploitative system is designed to keep the girl in the sex industry as long as possible.

Most of these women are illiterate. And those procured from neighbouring countries or the hill tribes cannot understand the local language. If they are lucky they may find a few women of their ethnic group in the same brothel, but when newly recruited they are unable to converse with their clients. Furthermore, their illegal status and the fear of deportation deters them from using governmental health services. In the North, near the border with Burma, Burmese prostitutes deported from Thailand are said to have disappeared without trace: rumours have circulated that they were executed by the Burmese authorities, who feared they would spread HIV within the country.

Beyond the brothel

The Public Health Ministry has an even more ambitious target for its "condom campaign": the use of condoms by the population as a whole, in both casual and marital sex. The ultimate goal is to distribute 120 million condoms annually to cover the number of sexual acts calculated to occur throughout the country.

In the case of casual sex, distribution is a challenge. "Unlike introducing condoms into the sex establishments, here we don't know when and where casual sex occurs," Dr Kunasol comments. Making condoms available in hotel toilets is one possible strategy.

Thailand's recent economic boom has partly contributed to the spread of HIV. Young workers have migrated in hordes to work in the mushrooming factories and service industries in Bangkok, leaving behind their families and traditional moral codes. Sexual encounters are commonplace among teenage migrants. In a factory operating 24 hours a day, Somchai works alongside 5,000 young women, mostly teenagers, and casual sex between rural girls and their male co-workers is not uncommon. "It is fashionable for a girl to have a boyfriend in the same workplace," Somchai says. "And it is equally fashionable for a man to have three different girlfriends at a time, who work three different shifts daily."

Somchai knows he is HIV-positive, but has not told his co-workers who feel the virus is remote. Indeed, Nittaya Prompawcheunboon, director of the AIDS programme of the Duang Prateep Foundation, says most men have the impression that AIDS is a make-believe disease—because those pronounced HIV-positive five or six years ago are still physically healthy and strong.

A sensitive issue

"For marital sex [condom use] is a most sensitive issue," says Dr Kunasol. "Recommending condoms between married couples could break what is left of an already fragile trust. Discreet strategies must be initiated," he says. Even women well informed about HIV and how it spreads rarely discuss safer sex with husbands who have other partners. "My husband said condoms are for prostitutes not for wives," one woman says.

According to Nittaya Prompawcheunboon, "When some housewives raise the topic of condom use with their husbands, it may come to blows instead. The husband would doubt his wife's faithfulness, leading to domestic violence."

Since the unequal standards of sexual behaviour make women extremely vulnerable to HIV infection from partners, and since couples wanting children must have unprotected sex, many feel that a key element in HIV/AIDS campaigns has to be the challenging of men's assumed right to unlimited sexual activity at the expense of their wives.

Until attitudes change, women have a limited range of options to protect their sexual health. Sombhong Pattwichaiporn, executive director of the Planned Parenthood Association of Thailand (PPAT), says: "I have seen the wife of a civil servant pack her husband's luggage for a brief business trip, and include condoms." He believes that one reason is the perpetuation of stereotypes by the older generation, which encourage the dependency of women. They were taught to be perfect housewives, and always to submit themselves to the boss of the house. In traditional literature a hero is synonymous with a womaniser.

"It would help to educate women in the new generation about their sexuality, their rights and their reproductive health," says Dr Kunasol. Sex education for the formal curriculum is being drafted. "Apart from the formal school system, sexuality will also be included in non-formal education which reaches people especially in remote rural areas," he says. Over two million people are currently registered for informal education.

Education campaigns need to be targeted at men and women. Some AIDS workers are keen to promote a "one partner for life" doctrine. But Jon Ungphakorn insists on a more realistic approach: "Preaching alone won't help.... Reducing the number of partners and using condoms are strategies people can adopt." He believes it is important to build a positive attitude to sex, which for many is characterised by guilt and lack of confidence. People in rural communities in particular suffer from lack of privacy: sex has to be restrained, noiseless and in the dark. "Instead of a guilt-ridden feeling, we have to recreate their self-confidence, so that they won't need to explore sex in secret," he says.

Empowerment

Government education services leave numerous gaps, and the work of NGOs is also crucial, especially in reaching remote and underprivileged groups. Under the guidance of an NGO, a support group called Women Against AIDS (WAA) has been established in Sanpatong district in Chiang Mai, an area which promises visitors majestic scenery, fine weather and the sex services of beautiful women, and which has the second highest number of AIDS cases in the country. WAA is encouraging wives to voice their opinions and increase their bargaining power.

The biggest obstacle is the deep-rooted male dominance in the community. Fathers "can literally sell their daughters into the sex industry," says Ben Svasti Thomson, an NGO worker. Such an action is likely to be driven by deep poverty, but in some cases it may be prompted by the desire for a luxury item such as a motorcycle or a colour television. Children are regarded as the property of their parents and are expected to pay something back for their parents' care. The sense of obligation is strong and deep-rooted: many girls feel proud that sexual labour provides a better living for their aged parents back home. But as knowledge about AIDS spreads, some families have decided to keep their young girls away from the sex industry.

Various efforts are being made to curtail the influx of girls into the sex industry. The Education Ministry offers scholarships for girls finishing compulsory education at the age of 12 or 13. In 1994, during the school vacation, the ministry organised an educational tour to bring northern school girls to Bangkok; one local newspaper claimed the object was to remove the girls from villages during the peak time for "recruitment" into the sex industry.

The northern branch of the grassroots organisation Empower in Chiang Mai has inveigled its way into the massage parlours and brothels, where illiterate, minority and immigrant women live in cramped environments, under slave-like conditions. Trapped by debt, they are not free to participate in activities outside the brothels, so Empower brings lessons to them. "By guiding them into proper health care through education, we believe that we will restore their self-confidence," says Chitlada Rattanaphan, a coordinator for Empower. "That will eventually lead them to find the bargaining power to protect themselves."

In face of all the obstacles to AIDS prevention among women, Rattanaphan of Empower and Ben Svasti Thomson of Women Against AIDS, share a common belief about how to achieve safer sex: shift contraceptive control from men to women by making female condoms or vaginal virucidal cream available to them. "We hope that technology will find an appropriate safe sex tool for women soon. But by that time it may be too late for the rage of the disease," says Thomson.

Female condoms are not yet available in Thailand, and effective virucides which do not have side-effects have not yet been developed. Dr Kunasol of the CDC department is dubious. The country should be self-reliant and not technologically dependent, he says. He warns against commercial exploitation creating "false hopes" of technology that has not yet been proved effective.

Discrimination against women

In spite of education to reduce discrimination, there is a lingering desire to blame someone for the epidemic—prostitutes, particularly female ones, bear the brunt of this. Rattanaphan in Chiang Mai feels the bias emanates not only from the public, but also from government officials. "With the prejudiced belief that sex workers spread HIV, most public health officials have a negative approach towards the sex workers." Such attitudes only aggravate problems, she adds.

Nationwide, over one hundred anonymous clinics offer blood tests for HIV—mostly to men and female sex workers. "Questions posed to those who test HIV-positive imply promiscuity or prostitution contexts, and would drive many well-educated middle-class women underground," says Ornanong Intarajit, director of Hot Line counselling service. Poorer women are more likely to tolerate abuse and hostility, simply because they have fewer choices—and are more likely to need financial or psychological help. Middle-class women won't expose themselves: they tend to avoid the clinics and are more likely to seek information from hotline services, books or newspapers. If they are HIV-positive, they are most likely to find out when pregnant—from blood tests during ante-natal care.

Abortion dilemmas

In general, hospitals routinely test the blood of pregnant woman for HIV without the protection of anonymity, despite the Public Health Ministry's policy of no testing without consent. "The Public Health Ministry has never had any policy to test for HIV among pregnant women," says Dr Jamroon Mikhanorn, former ministry spokesman, adding, "In practice, doctors do not fully inform pregnant women of the government's policy [and] their rights."

Worse still, several hospitals do not have appropriate pre-test, or post-test counselling services. Of those that do, some are inclined to "directive counselling methods", which strongly recommend abortion to any woman found HIV-positive.

Barely three months into their marriage, Porn and Somsak (assumed names) were delighted by the news of Porn's pregnancy. The elation of parenthood quickly evaporated when Porn's blood test showed HIV-positive. Abortion was immediately recommended. Basic information about HIV and AIDS was explained, but the emphasis of the counselling was on how the child would become an orphan, if lucky enough to escape the one-in-three chance of infection. A dreadful future was painted to the stunned Porn.

Several couples, including Porn and Somsak, who visited public hospitals, told AIDS counsellors at Hot Line and Access that doctors and nurses persuaded them to consent to abortion. Some were not informed of the chance their babies had of surviving the infection.

"I was told abortion is the best solution," says Kanda recalling her first ante-natal visit at Bamrajnaradul Hospital in Bangkok. "They told me I am not going to live long and my child may have AIDS, get sick and eventually die. If he survives, he will be an orphan when my husband and I die."

A social worker at a government hospital who wishes to remain anonymous charges that "well-intentioned doctors often ignore human rights in their zeal for a medical solution, by forcing pregnant women to undergo blood tests, abortions and sterilisation."

Suchitra Wuthithamrong, a counsellor at Access, says that medical personnel often put too much emphasis on a patient's physical health, at the expense of his or her psychological wellbeing. "It is painful for any couple to be pressured into [abortion] right after they are told they have AIDS."

It has been obvious for quite some time that hospital and social systems are not prepared to handle even today's babies with AIDS, and AIDS orphans. Early abortion is seen by many doctors as one solution to the problem of pregnancy-related transmission.

While abortion is effectively illegal in Thailand, except in narrow circumstances of foetal malformation, rape or incest, or where it threatens the life or health of the mother, the AIDS epidemic has seen a relaxation in enforcement of the law. According to Dr Kobchitt Limpaphayom, head of Chulalongkorn Hospital's obstetrics and gynaecology department, "We know that what we've been doing is against the law.... And not everyone agrees with us, but we feel it is our duty to do this because of the possibly tremendous impact AIDS could have on society."

Compromises on abortion are not new. In the past, the desire to bring down Thailand's population growth to an average rate of two children per family, led to abortions sometimes being granted to couples with unwanted third pregnancies.

Dr Kobchitt insists that fewer than 1,000 abortions are done in hospitals each year. For her, "Abortion can prevent children from facing a grim future and the country from the burden of the enormous health expenses.... It's easy to talk about a child's right to be born and to be well taken care of. But in reality, who will take care of them? Will the human rights advocates do it?" In fact, says Kobchitt, babies with AIDS suffer until they die, and those who lose their parents are shunned and neglected due to existing prejudice against orphans—adoption is more acceptable if the child is a relative. People consider abandoned children to be offspring of the "bad blood" of society.

Dr Kobchitt denies allegations of directive counselling at her hospital. Her counsellors would never force or put pressure on patients to have abortions, she says, "We give them choices."

Giving counselling to HIV-positive pregnant women and their partners is extremely difficult. Helping couples to make such a painful decision can make it hard not to have doubts about the best approach. "The extent of the problem of orphans and infected infants is already so serious that some of us have had second thoughts that straight counselling truly helps women and their children," says Piengjai Sudtho, a hospital social counsellor.

While public hospitals are criticised for encouraging abortion, Catholic hospitals hold fast to their religion's ban on abortion and urge pregnant women to take the risk and carry the pregnancy to term, says Dr Suporn Kerdsawang, a consultant at Siriraj Hospital's health research centre. He says counsellors should provide as much information as possible, and with enough information patients will be able to make the decision that is best suited to them.

Niramol said she and her husband agreed to carry on with the pregnancy and to take the risk with their child. "It's our child, how could we terminate it?"

Sri in Chiang Mai decided to keep the pregnancy because she is confident that her family, though poor, would pitch in to ease the financial burden of bringing up the child.

Yuang wanted to abort the foetus, but her husband insisted he needed the baby. She went ahead with the pregnancy. He promised to take responsibility for the expenses of looking after the child and providing savings should both parents die.

Keo sensed strong discrimination against people with AIDS in her village. If she and her husband died, their child would lead a miserable life in the village all alone, if it escaped infection. She and her husband decided in favour of an abortion.

Wan and Pote come from a well-off family and Pote's parents yearn for descendants to inherit their wealth. They chose to take the chance.

From sex to sterilisation

Right after abortion or delivery, most HIV-positive women are sterilised. It is rarer for the man to be sterilised. There is criticism that sterilisation, too, is pressured. Dr Prapan Phanuphak, director of the Thai Red Cross programme on AIDS, while agreeing that abortion is a legitimate solution for many women and couples, objects to the fact that many men and women have been coerced into accepting sterilisation. Even if they elect for sterilisation, he says, doctors should refrain from permanently sterilising them, because of the chance, however slim, that a cure or treatment may be found and the patients may want to have babies again.

Thus HIV makes reproductive and sexual choices, from sexual intercourse to sterilisation, critically difficult for men and women—but particularly so for women, who also bear the brunt of the consequences. Dealing with this is not easy, especially in a country which is used to overlooking women's perspectives. HIV control campaigns might look different if they truly reflected women's concerns and women were involved in designing them.

In order to address women's concerns, HIV has to be seen much more as a reproductive issue, not just a sexual health problem. The overwhelming majority of Thai men and women want to marry and have children. All the time they are trying to conceive they are having unprotected sex. In any unprotected sex, the physiological risks of HIV transmission are up to two times higher from men to women than vice versa [15].

To avoid the situation where any sex to conceive is worryingly unsafe, new expectations of sexual behaviour do have to be forged. But these expectations must go beyond condom use, they need to embrace changes in the balance of sexual power, currently so much in men's favour—which ultimately means there must be shifts in the balance of social and economic power.

HIV is not merely an issue of sexual health but jeopardises the survival of families. This message could be a powerful incentive to behavioural change—but real attitudinal change would mean the acceptance of equal responsibilities and rights for men and women.

Room to Decide

Education, employment and reproductive choice in Pakistan

By Ayesha Khan

It is widely assumed that women who are educated and generate their own income, gain higher status within the family and have fewer children. In turn, this is believed to improve the quality of women's lives. However, demographers and family planning advocates are discovering that the problem of how to improve women's status is more complex than it first seemed.

Although research suggests that there is a link between the education and employment of women and having smaller families, there are mixed conclusions about whether wage employment actually increases a woman's status and decision-making power within the family [1].

A study in Pakistan found that educated women have fewer children partly because they marry later and also because their wish to educate their own children makes it too great an economic burden to have a large family [2]. The study claimed that employment alone does not indicate an improvement in a woman's position, unless it is in a higher status job such as teaching or medicine. Poorer women are more likely to work out of necessity than choice and their employment in lower status jobs does little to improve their own status.

Another, Karachi-based, study found that women in higher status jobs have almost half the completed family size of those working in lower status jobs [3]. Another found that women with higher status ratings discussed family size more often with their spouses [4].

Clearly, efforts are underway to identify the factors which allow women to control the size of their families and improve their status. But as researcher Zeba Sathar observes, the term "status" is hard to define. Does having fewer children actually indicate greater decision-making power and autonomy for a woman? Is it not possible that lowered fertility rates indicate a quantitative, but not necessarily a qualitative, change in women's lives?

The following extracts from interviews reveal what 10 Pakistani women consider to be the extent of their own decision-making powers and the constraints under which their decisions are made. They show too that for these women, most of whom are considered privileged in terms of class, employment and level of education, reproductive decisionmaking is inextricable from other aspects of their lives. As one of them clearly states, reproductive choice is only truly a choice when women have "room to decide", and are not hemmed in by social structures which leave them little room to manoeuvre.

"For the sake of marriage"

When women in Pakistan try to study, they often have their first lesson in how limited their control is over their own lives. Literacy rates do not tell us about the battles fought within families and communities to allow even 22% of Pakistan's women access to some form of schooling. Education statistics, which reveal that only 12% of women make it to secondary school and 3% to the tertiary level, indicate that the fight for education does not get any easier for women, even of the middle and upper classes, as they advance beyond more basic levels.

Anisa, one of the few Pakistani women whose parents allowed her to complete a master's degree is not exceptional among her peers when she admits: "If a proper proposal came, I was ready to leave my studies." In her conservative family, marriages are arranged for girls by the age of 21. The major reason Anisa was allowed to study was because no decent proposal had arrived.

"I didn't socialise. I wasn't such a stunning beauty that people would spot me at wedding functions. I wasn't encouraging anyone because I thought my father would shoot me if I brought a proposal from the university.... But I was desperate to get married. I was under pressure from my relatives who said: 'How unfortunate! What a pity! She is unwanted.' They would offer to help and suggest someone really, really bad just to show what they thought I was worth."

Room to Decide   123

Only 12% of girls in Pakistan receive secondary school education.

Finally, Anisa asked her parents to find her someone. "I didn't want to meet the man." She only requested that he should not be poor and that he should at least have a bachelor's degree. A husband was found, but after her marriage Anisa was made to stay in the house against her will. "It was unthinkable to leave the house unescorted." Her single attempt to enrol on a computer course didn't stand a chance: "I said I wanted to learn computers at an institute opposite the house. He said, 'You aren't even taking care of the house well, how can you think of computers?'"

Nasifa's parents and aunt arranged her marriage at the age of 21 to her cousin, before she had completed her master's degree. The marriage to her cousin was arranged by her parents and aunt. "I tried to convey my reservations but was persuaded," says Nasifa. "I accepted this decision because I had led a very protected life where all decisions had been made for me." The earlier option of a master's degree had been suggested to Nasifa by her parents, who fully supported the notion of a highly educated daughter—provided that she fulfilled her social obligation to marry at the appropriate time.

But higher education had instilled some ambition in Nasifa: "I knew I was going to complete my degree even before my *shadi* [wedding]. I agreed to marry on condition that I would take only one semester off."

Her in-laws strongly resented her decision to return to university one year later without her husband: "They thought I was being too independent...it would give the impression that I have the power to make these decisions and my husband must be weak." She also had to contend with vicious gossip from within the community, alleging that she was unable to make her marriage work. Today, at 29, she says: "It is the one achievement of my life that I have done [my degree]."

Fouzia, a lawyer and mother of three, married just after completing her bachelor's degree. She and her husband knew and liked each other before their engagement. Further study was always a priority with Fouzia and she soon enrolled on a law course. But her husband wanted them to spend more time together as they had only recently married. "I wanted to study. I didn't agree, but I had to quit it for the sake of my marriage."

Fouzia's first pregnancy was also for the sake of her marriage. Since she had stopped studying and her husband wanted a baby, she complied. After a few more years of marriage, her husband no longer minded her plans to study, and her second child was born while she was doing her law degree.

"I've enjoyed having children.... It has been a great experience for me, at least.... Only [waiting longer for] the first one might have changed my life—I might have been more qualified and educated."

Fouzia has very clear ideas on reproductive choice, which she says is a question of spacing and timing. "The decision should be made by both the partners, but it should be more the woman's choice because in our society the woman bears full responsibility for bringing up a child."

Marriage and education are closely intertwined. Anisa, Nasifa and Fouzia belong to a privileged class: their university years coincided with the early years of marriage, so education became controversial at this stage. For women from the rural areas, the issue of education usually has meaning at the primary school level only. After marriage, which takes place at puberty, education is no longer a possibility.

Shamim is the first girl in her entire extended family to gain an education. Her father is a plumber who moved to Islamabad for work and built a small house for his family in an illegal squatter area. Shamim went to a government school for eight years. "In my family of Pathans, it is considered a sin to educate girls. My father is the only one who did because he himself is educated. My relatives have kept a distance from him for this reason." She had to drop her education when it was time to get married, in her case at the age of 15.

A woman's first duty

At the time of her marriage Shamim was ignorant about sex and about family planning. Her first child was born 10 months later, and none of her pregnancies was planned. When she found herself pregnant for the third time she went to a woman in a nearby village who offered her some "medicine" to cause a miscarriage. But Shamim could not afford the 55 rupees (about US$1) the woman asked for. "If I had had the money myself, without having to ask for anything from anybody, then I would have bought those pills.... My mind is ready now. If I could do something differently I would have spaced my children more."

Now 25, Shamim acknowledges that she wants to take more control of her life because of the changes she has undergone since she began working a few years ago, after her third son was born. Her job, with the adult literacy and basic healthcare programmes of a local women's organisation, has raised her status in the community. She recalls that she used to sneak out of her house to attend work meetings because her in-laws forbade her to go out on her own. To this day her husband only lets her work because he believes she does not meet or speak to any men.

Work has made her aware of herself as an individual with her own needs. "Before, all I thought about was cooking and things like that, never about changing my life at home. I never asked anything from anyone except my mother, not even my husband. I didn't know where the world was!"

At the same time, her responsibilities at home have increased—she has recently had a fourth child. Shamim, who has broken away from her expected social role and is working outside the home, feels overwhelmed and worn out. Despite the economic and personal benefits she derives from being employed, Shamim says: "I think it is easier for those women who stay at home."

Shamim's story typifies a contradiction in the experience of women, across the class spectrum, who have been brought up with a strict definition of what their future roles ought to be and who have since developed an awareness beyond that. Often they experience disappointment, which can border on depression, when they realise that their personal aspirations are unlikely to be fulfilled.

Shazia is a member of the educated elite class which wields most of the power in Pakistan. Her parents permitted her to complete her master's degree before having the mandatory arranged marriage. She accepted this form of marriage, intending to begin a career afterwards. When, just a few months after the birth of her first child, she discovered she was pregnant again, her plans became impossible. She considered an abortion but realised she was too timid to take the decision herself. "I wanted someone else to convince me to have an abortion." When nobody did, she hoped for a miscarriage. "I wanted God to get rid of this because I wasn't courageous enough to get it done myself."

The decision to keep the child was consistent with the approach she had taken towards all the major choices in her life, in which she had not resisted the strong force of family or social obligation. To Shazia, reproductive choice is only possible if you are "important enough that somebody gives you room to decide".

For this reason she says: "Circumstances should be created so that women can handle the responsibility and have the confidence to choose. It would involve what you think of yourself, your relationship with your husband—how much importance he attaches to what you say and think, and what position you have in the house where you go after marriage. It is about how much confidence and trust everybody around you is willing to put in you."

The case of Mehreen stands in dramatic contrast to Shazia's and illustrates how differently a woman can handle her reproductive capabilities if decision-making power has been nurtured in her. After being educated in a top private school she won a scholarship to do her bachelor's degree abroad. Her family's confidence in her ability to live on her own and determine her own course of study sets her experience apart from that of most Pakistani women.

After returning to Pakistan, Mehreen began working. At the age of 25, later than many of her peers, she married a man of her own choice. At 30, she has not yet had a child. "If I didn't have such a demanding and fulfilling job I might have decided to have a child earlier," she says.

Early on in her marriage she became pregnant by accident and decided, after discussion with her husband, to have an abortion. She is now conscious of pressure from her own parents to have a child, and the fact that the time for healthy childbearing is not unlimited. Still, she says: "I will have a child when I have accomplished something in life, feel I can take a break, and feel that both my husband and myself really want a child."

Women like Mehreen, who demonstrate relatively greater control over their lives, are given little credit by society. The terms in which women speak of each other is revealing. If a husband listens to his wife, she is "lucky". If she goes out to work, it means he "gives" her freedom. If she is mobile, it is because he "lets" her roam about "freely". The underlying message is clear: a woman can never be the active decisionmaker in her own life.

Right to divorce

Anisa's experience of restricted choice within marriage did not end with her husband's blocking of her computer course. She also found him unwilling to let her delay childbearing. Her story demonstrates how a woman can be made to feel incompetent to make decisions herself in the face of society's pressures. After her wedding, she made one attempt to control her own fertility: "I knew I could postpone a child by using contraceptives—I didn't because my husband didn't allow me to. I didn't have support, or the courage to discuss it with someone. With the first child everybody believes you should leave it to Allah, and use something only with the second child."

When her husband realised she wanted to use contraception, he told his mother, who was deeply offended at her daughter in-law's "suspicious" behaviour.

Anisa was horrified to find herself pregnant after one month of marriage to a man she disliked from the start. Her husband's family had lied when they said he had an MBA from Europe. In reality he wished to extract a high dowry from her family.

"I wanted to have an abortion. I couldn't talk to my mother about it, to no one." She remembered vivid scenes of desperate heroines in Pakistani films, and half-heartedly tried to throw herself down the stairs. "I had this basic disappointment. Even if I had an abortion...there was...no way out." When she eventually separated from her husband, it was he who dumped her in fury back at her parents' house.

At the time of Anisa's marriage, the *nikahnama* (marriage contract) provided only for her husband to have the automatic right to divorce. According to Pakistani law, a man may give his wife this same right at the time of signing the *nikahnama*. Most Pakistani women are unaware that this is possible, and parents do not insist for fear of insulting the groom and his family. This is why most women in Pakistan have no automatic right of divorce and must resort to long and expensive court battles in order to free themselves from marriages like Anisa's.

Balancing acts

Women in Pakistan, divided along ethnic and class lines, have a shared experience of patriarchy, a structure in which men wield the major decision-making power and women's role is determined by and limited to their reproductive and nurturing capacities. If they do attain some control over decisionmaking, they find it extremely difficult to balance all their aspirations with their responsibilities, and incorporate motherhood smoothly into their lives, or incorporate employment and study plans into their role as mothers.

Nasifa has one child. She is likely to have another in the next few years because she wants to complete her family before the age of 30 and because of pressure from her husband, mother-in-law and sister-in-law. "If it was only for my sake, I wouldn't have another child, but my daughter needs one and my husband wants at least two. But I don't feel anything missing in my life."

Her main concern is the effect that having another child would have on her job, having fought so hard to complete her master's degree after marriage. She began work only when her daughter started going to play-school. She has a career-track position in a company, with flexible working hours that allow her to be home for her daughter.

Nasifa would be happy if she managed to keep her present job with the arrival of a second child. Marriage and motherhood have altered her career ambitions somewhat. "I want to progress," she says, "but at the same time not at the cost of having to neglect my family or my home.... My daughter is the biggest joy of my life."

If quantitative data on the effect of women's education and employment on fertility rates were being collected, it would be easy to conclude that a woman like Nasifa is a success story. She is unlikely to have more than two children; she and her husband use contraceptives; her qualifications and formal sector employment grant her high status in society; and she does not rely on a large number of children for security. But from Nasifa's perspective, control over her life and its important decisions has been hard-won and the fight is not over. Even today, as soon as she has achieved a balance between motherhood and career, the pressure is on to reproduce again.

The way in which women talk about their lives reveals how complicated, and often draining, is the balancing act between study, marriage, job and children. To pursue an education in the first place requires the sanction of a woman's family, and to use that qualification for employment needs to be balanced with the demands of her family.

Working for survival

"I kill myself working. I have to clean 20 rooms a day, every day." This is the reality for women like Huma, a sweeper at a girls' school in Islamabad, who are at the bottom of the socio-economic hierarchy. She and her husband are economic migrants from the countryside.

Huma is illiterate. No one in her family has ever been to school. Married at the age of 16 to a stranger chosen by her parents and with no knowledge of modern contraceptive methods, she bore four children, had two stillbirths and one miscarriage. In the village, her mother-in-law used to insist that Huma give her son 14 children—as many as she had borne herself. Huma says coming to the city saved her from that fate. She admits she and her husband now know how to avoid having more children but will not disclose the details.

While she was caring for her four children at home, she knew her husband, also a sweeper, shouldered a heavy economic burden: "But my husband didn't let me work. He said, 'God has given life and I will earn. When you stop having children then you can work.'"

Huma began work the day her youngest son started school, six years ago. Her main concern was to save enough money to marry off her eldest daughter, which has now been achieved. Huma's job doesn't raise her low status: it is a reflection of it. She works out of economic necessity, to support her family. Millions of other Pakistani women, struggling to provide for many children, are similarly driven to join the workforce.

Bano was married before puberty and sent from her village to live with her husband's family in a village near Islamabad. For two years, she continued to live as a child. "I used to make dolls' clothes with the material left over from my husband's tailoring job."

Soon after their sexual relations began, she had two children in quick succession. Her mother-in-law insisted that she avoid a third pregnancy too soon. Bano was too frightened to use modern contraceptive methods, so she and her husband established a system of abstaining from sex for 20 days following each menstruation. Although there have been two more children, both have been after a gap of three years. Bano says her husband's cooperation is not out of consideration for her, but because she is insistent. "My husband doesn't care how many children we have. He believes God grants livelihood. I am the one who insists on doing something to avoid pregnancy because I have to labour to support the ones we already have, and don't want any more."

Bano went to work as a midwife and massage-woman while her fourth child was still an infant and the other three were attending school. Her husband tolerates her working, but whenever he feels she is becoming too opinionated he tells her to quit. She deeply resents him. "I do everything for my husband and his children. After all, I left my own home, my own family, to be married to him. But if there is any difference in the housework, if his dinner is even slightly late, then he curses me and tells me that I have to quit my job."

Bano has assumed some control over her reproductive decisionmaking for two reasons: her in-laws have supported her, and she is so desperate economically that she does not want more children. She feels that working has made little difference to her status within her husband's family. "If my husband had been able to support us himself he wouldn't have let me work."

Education for independence

Rubina, a widow of 44, was born in a mountain region in the north of Pakistan and is a Pathan. Schooling was never an option for her—"Our people's girls don't go to school," she says—and employment only became possible later in life when she needed to support her family.

At the age of 12, she was married to a tailor friend of the family who was somewhere between 60 and 65. She bore him six children. Rubina remembers that there were no discussions with her husband about limiting the size of their family. Moreover, she says: "What Allah sends into this world he provides for. We should not interfere. Now as a widow, what would I be without my children?" Although she claims that she does not believe family planning is a bad thing, she has little faith in its efficacy. "What Allah has to send, no person has the strength to stop."

When they moved to the city and her children enrolled in schools, Rubina learned basic reading and writing skills from them. Her husband taught her to sew and she has worked as a seamstress since he died. Today all her children have completed high school, including her only daughter. "I thought the world is a more difficult place for a woman," she explains. "A man at least can work. If a girl is educated, then she can have an honourable life. Girls' education is even more important than boys'." Unusually, Rubina believes that a girl should marry between 25 and 30 years of age: "She will be more intelligent. She can look after her house and her in-laws better, and fight less than I did."

Rabia, a middle-class woman with a bachelor's degree, says: "If a woman works and is independent, then she has the option to leave her husband if they fight. She has a base. But here in Pakistan she cannot go back to her family, because they usually can't afford to keep her. A husband here wants to be the only one to earn. If the wife does, then he can't think of her as a slave any more."

Rabia has watched closely the experience of her sister, now unhappily expecting her fifth child and allowed very little freedom by her husband. "My sister's husband considers her the servant to him, the house, and their children," she observes.

Rabia sees herself as different from other women in her community because she is strong-willed and is not married to a controlling husband. "I always wanted a man who would protect, honour, listen to me, look after me if he was older. My husband does give a lot of importance to what women say." The reason she gives for the importance of economic independence—that it allows a

132 *Private Decisions, Public Debate*

"The world is a more difficult place for a woman....If a girl is educated, then she can have an honourable life." (Rubina, 44-year-old widow, married at 12)

woman to leave her husband if she needs to—is not something she has had to apply to her own life. When her children are older, she would like to do some voluntary social work.

Reproductive choice: life choices

The message heard in the voices of these women is that they do want to have control over if and when to have children and how many to have. They demonstrate it repeatedly by searching for ways to achieve this in balance with other aspects of their lives, over which they also do not have enough control.

The difficulties encountered in resisting being forced into a passive role over major decisions will be familiar to all Pakistani women; none of these women's stories is unusual. But most women's experience remains private, and only when their stories are brought out into the open and analysed collectively, is the common thread so striking. This is particularly disquieting for women from privileged backgrounds who are accustomed to viewing uneducated and poor women as the ones truly lacking in control over their destinies and who often perceive themselves as cushioned from the harsher realities of male dominance in Pakistan. More rigid social norms in the upper classes, which discourage women from sharing confidences outside the family, also encourage the myth that privileged women are not victimised by patriarchal norms.

Reproductive choice is a part of the larger life pattern, and the struggle for this freedom is inseparable from the struggle to make other choices—to study, to work, to stay single, to marry but remain independent, to develop a career, to plan a family. As the women interviewed make abundantly clear, improving women's status is far from a simple matter: although lowered fertility rates may be taken as one example of the way in which education and employment alter women's lives, the assumption that it necessarily indicates improved control over reproductive decision-making is a glib one.

At the international level, human rights advocates have also expressed their concern that women's "reproductive rights" should not be isolated from the larger context of women's issues. A briefing paper prepared by the Center for Reproductive Law and Policy, New York, argues:

> Regulation of women's reproductive function is effectuated through unwritten social norms as well as through government laws and policies. Laws as diverse as those regulating marriage and divorce, maternity leave, economic discrimination, employment, eligibility for free or low cost health care, and domestic violence or sexual abuse—as well as laws explicitly ensuring informed consent or restricting reproductive options—all affect the status of women and

whether they are empowered to effectuate reproductive control over their lives. Governments must pledge to oppose laws and policies that obstruct or fail adequately to guarantee access to reproductive health and choice [5].

The inability of governments and organisations to make the kind of commitment urged here stems from their policy standpoint. Women's control over their own fertility is a goal sought by feminists, activists and policymakers alike, but often for very different reasons. The achievement of women's health, including control over fertility, is a profoundly different policy objective from that of reducing population growth rates. In either case, it is an error to discuss women's reproductive control without exploring all the other forms of control which they are lacking. Failure to look at the wider context explains the frustration of the family planning worker who cannot comprehend why a woman may be unable to practise responsible family planning even if various contraceptive methods are available to her.

The women interviewed show that they already know that reproductive choice is deeply intertwined with other important life choices. As Shazia said: "You have to be important enough that somebody gives you room to decide." It can safely be said that in Pakistan almost every woman experiences a debilitating sense of her own unimportance, and is largely unfamiliar with the elusive "space" in which to decide most things for herself.

We Can't Stop Now

Pakistan and the politics of reproduction

By Hilda Saeed

> *Mein to chali re*
> *Aeri sakhion be' deswa*
> *Apni sahelion se dur*
> *Babui ke galiyon se dur...dur*
>
> *I am going far away*
> *Away from the country of my loved ones*
> *Away from my friends and my people*
> *Away from my home*

The week-long wedding celebrations draw to a close, and the traditional song—sung when the bride leaves her parents' home—drifts out of the colourful *shamiana* (tent). The bride, Samina, is only 15 years old.

Rukhsati, the time of a bride's departure, is an emotionally charged moment. "But what can we do?" asks a guest. "That is the way of the world. It is fate. But thank Allah, the parents have disposed of their *bojh* [burden] with honour." Blessings are showered upon the young woman as she leaves with her bridegroom: "May you be the mother of many sons."

A lifetime of childbearing

If she is lucky, a Pakistani woman will be married in her late teens or early twenties—a trend which is growing. But many girls, especially in rural areas, are married in their early teens or at an even younger age—10, nine or sometimes eight. A lifetime of childbearing stretches before them.

Demographic experts fear that young women like Samina, with little say in deciding the number of their children, will inevitably add to the nightmare of Pakistan's exploding population. The country's population is estimated to be 120 million (the last census was completed in 1981, the next expected to begin in late 1994). It is estimated to be growing at an annual rate of 3.2%, faster than anywhere else in the world [1].

Since the 1960s, billions of dollars have been spent on containing population growth, but to little effect: only a quarter of the population has access to family planning services. The younger and more recently married the wife, the less likely she is to have access to contraception—which is most commonly used after women have had four, six or even eight children.

Only 6% of rural women currently use contraception, compared with 31% in cities. Likewise, use ranges from 8% among women with no schooling to 38% among those with at least some secondary education.

A tragic result of women's lack of access to contraception is the suffering caused by incomplete abortion. The Jinnah Postgraduate Medical Centre in Karachi treats an average of 1,500 cases a year of complications arising from illegal abortion. According to the Pakistani Penal Code, abortion by any method and for any reason other than to save the life of the woman is illegal; in the rare cases of medical abortion, the woman is questioned by a panel of experts.

Dr Freny Cowasjee, consultant gynaecologist and obstetrician at Karachi's Holy Family Hospital, comments: "The whole situation is shrouded in secrecy: we know it [illegal abortion] occurs because of the clinical complications, but are helpless to stop it, because the patients never admit anything. The women who have abortions are invariably married, with six, eight, or even 10 children. The abortion is invariably the last desperate resort, and the tragedy is that if only birth control measures were widely available, this need not even happen."

"A notable failure"

During the 30 years of formal commitment to family planning services, the major share of national funds has been channelled to defence and debt servicing, now absorbing 28% and 17% of GNP respectively [2]. Meanwhile, funding for the social sector has been woefully inadequate, as evidenced by standard indicators: the national literacy rate is 26.6% and female literacy 16% [3]; the infant mortality rate is 94 deaths per 1,000 live births, and the maternal mortality rate five per 1,000 live births—20 per 1,000 in the province of Baluchistan [4]. But since women have several children, the lifetime risk is much higher.

According to Dr Nafis Sadik, assistant secretary-general of the United Nations Population Fund (UNFPA): "Since 1971...the social sector has been completely neglected. The status of women is inextricably linked to...girls' education. A major constraint is the lack of health facilities and inaccessibility of health outlets... [5]". A major reason for failure, says Dr Sadik, is that family planning has been viewed as a demographic concern, rather than "an essential component of maternal and child health [6]".

This neglect is vividly illustrated by statistics on health facilities. According to one expert, "it is widely accepted that barely 10% of government-directed village health outlets are functional [7]." Furthermore, health and population are the concerns of separate ministries which until recently functioned separately but are now collaborating more closely. Nonetheless, women are hesitant about visiting family planning clinics. Rare is the woman who will attend a clinic without her husband, particularly in rural areas.

"Of course Pakistan is a notable failure," comments Kareem Iqbal, former federal secretary in the Ministry of Population Affairs, referring to family planning provision. "Constant political changes and adhoc-ism ruins the programme." He cites inadequate finance and inconsistency of approach as basic problems, as well as a failure to understand and involve the community: "Unless we understand the felt needs of the community and accord women a higher status, step up their literacy and employment, get away from son preference, we cannot succeed. There has to be male motivation as well. Just as war is too important a matter to be left to generals alone, so too population is everybody's concern."

Child mothers

"Something must be done for our women," says Ama, a respected elder and adviser to the women of Makii, a village in Sindh. "My life is over, but what have these poor innocents done to deserve this fate?" She points to five little girls, playing nearby. The eldest, a girl, is about 10, the youngest three. "My daughter-in-law, a lovely girl,

138 Private Decisions, Public Debate

Childhood for Pakistani girls is often brief; by their teens many are experiencing motherhood for real.

died in childbirth. I kept telling my son to take her to the city for an operation [tubal ligation], but he didn't. He wanted a son."

Khatoo, wife of a lorry driver in Karachi and mother of seven children, is forbidden by her husband to attend a family planning clinic: "My husband won't listen—he says he's earning enough, so why shouldn't he have as many children as he wants? Personally, I'd have been happy with two or three, so I could look after them properly."

In the village of Sanghar, in Sindh, Safia Bano says: "Sometimes the *dais* [birth attendants] are good, sometimes not. When there are problems, the pregnant woman has to be rushed to hospital in a bullock cart. They shoot from kalashnikov rifles, to make the bullock run faster, and to startle the woman into delivery."

The Child Marriage Restraint Act, which outlaws marriage below the age of 16, is ignored all over the country. Nanyan Bibi, mother of two daughters and six sons, lives on outskirts of the Punjab metropolis of Rawalpindi. With tears in her eyes she relates the story of her little girl, married at the age of six to a man of 60. "But my other daughter Zeenat—I'm not going to let her get married till she's at least 25," she says with quiet determination.

Early marriage means that young girls become mothers while they are still essentially children themselves. At 14, Bakht Bibi from Moosa Colony near Quetta, Baluchistan, still has the mischief of childhood in her eyes. Unbelievably, she is the mother of two, and five months pregnant with a third. "I pray to Allah", she confides, "that I may have no more children—but I'm scared too, because then my husband will take another wife."

Zar Gul, from the village of Kili in Baluchistan, is in her early twenties and has already given birth eight times (two of her children have died). "I was married at 10. I wasn't even *jawan* [had not reached puberty]. I don't want any more children, but he won't listen."

All over Pakistan—in rural areas and urban slums—the stories are the same. Everywhere, very young women have very low status and are expected to carry an intolerable burden and are denied any right to exercise reproductive choice. "Anaemia, early marriage, multiparity [many children]—all result in high-risk pregnancies," says Dr Sadiqua Jaffery, professor of gynaecology and obstetrics at Karachi's premier medical institute, the Jinnah Postgraduate Medical Centre. Not only is enormous physical stress experienced by young women in particular; the emotional cost exacted of them is also very high. Psychiatrist Unaiza Niaz and clinical psychologist Riffat Moazzam both speak of the high incidence of depression and other psychiatric illnesses among these women.

Violent extremes

Two-thirds of Pakistan's population live in rural areas where feudalism and tribalism are often entrenched. The *Zamindaar* (landowner) and tribal chieftain are the lords and masters; the *haris*, or land tenants, entirely at their mercy. Bonded labour exists in significant proportions, and has been taken up by the Human Rights Commission of Pakistan.

Some of the desperately poor manage to escape; others face a lifetime of endless human bondage. For women caught up in this, the question of reproductive choice is an unpermitted luxury. A raped woman is considered a dishonour to her family and community, so the kidnapping and raping of women is kept a secret, rather than challenged or reported. The Human Rights Commission of Pakistan reports that in 1993 a woman was raped every three hours (findings similar to those in other countries), and at least two were gang-raped every day of the year. Half of all those assaulted were minors or teenagers. A woman died of domestic violence every other day [8].

Some particularly extreme customs have evolved. In Sindh, *Bibi Saathis* (lady companions) belonging to wealthy families are "married" to the Qur'an so that their share of land does not leave the family [9]. Ritual murder, or *karo kari*, has been used as a means of eliminating an enemy by accusing him of adultery, and then ritually murdering him and the woman concerned—both are hacked to death. Originally only heard of in Baluchistan, *karo kari* has now been reported in Sindh and Punjab too. In these two provinces, there have been reports of insulting a man by stripping his womenfolk in public, and forcing them to dance naked in the streets.

Women activists all over the country have been up in arms against these shocking acts, which are punishable offences under the Pakistan Penal Code. Such events may not be frequent but under-reporting is likely. At least one or two incidents appear daily in the national press. Says Mariam Palijo, founder member of *Sindhiani Tehreek* (the Sindh women's rights organisation which is 15,000-strong): "Women are beaten up, forced to marry where the elders decide, treated like livestock. We have faced opposition everywhere, but we're fighting it. It isn't easy for women to get together even for a social visit, but we've struggled against those limitations, and are succeeding."

Politics and religion

Since Independence in 1947, Pakistan has had a turbulent history. Three wars with India, in 1948, 1965 and 1971, the separation of Bangladesh in 1971, and the war in neighbouring Afghanistan in the 1970s, all resulted in further impoverishment of an already chronically poor country—and worsened conditions for women. Nor has the political regime been conducive to the improvement of women's health and status. There have been long stretches of martial law, totalling over 20 years, of which that under military dictator Zia-ul-Haq was "especially harsh for women", says human rights and women's activist Anis Haroon.

"The Constitution was put into abeyance," she explains, "fundamental rights suspended, and a series of ordinances and laws were introduced—the Hudood Ordinances [Hudood is plural for *hadd*, or limit] and the Laws of Evidence—which legally reduced women's status to half that of a man's. Since, socially and traditionally, women were already subservient, you can well imagine what the atmosphere was like in those days—still is, in fact."

These discriminatory laws have been in force since 1979, even though they negate Article 25 of the Constitution, which guarantees equality irrespective of caste, sex or creed. "Unless such laws are repealed, women cannot get their due status. In all these years, barely two rapists have been punished, while over 1,000 women and girls are in jail under false charges of adultery," says Anis Haroon. The *Zina* (adultery) law, is part of the Hudood Ordinances. *Zina-bil-jabar* is the term for rape. According to Shariaa (Islamic law), a man can only be convicted of rape if there have been four adult Muslim witnesses to the rape. On the other hand, a woman's pregnancy is admitted as evidence of adultery. *Zina-bil-jabar* (rape) is changed by law enforcers to *Zina* (adultery) and the woman convicted.

The repressive and punitive ethos of the Zia years had a profound effect on women. Even educated women internalised it. "It's amazing," comments a feminist. "The effect has been insidious— even I find myself covering up carefully with a large *dupatta* [long scarf] as if my body is something to be ashamed of—and I used to go around in sleeveless blouses."

Orthodox behavioural codes, not so apparent at the time of Independence, gained ground in the 1970s and 1980s and continue to be influential. *Purdah* (the veil) and the segregation of women are seen as ideal Islamic practices, particularly in the urban middle class. Rural women generally do not observe *purdah*, but roles are strictly defined according to gender and segregation is common.

Following General Zia's death in 1988, three democratic governments have been dissolved and three caretaker governments installed, causing repeated turmoil. The Pakistan People's Party, under Benazir Bhutto—daughter of a former leader, Zulfikar Ali Bhutto—formed the first democratic government after Zia, but lasted barely one and a half years. It was re-elected in October 1993. The current government is regarded as the first "woman-friendly" one in recent years but there are concerns over President Bhutto's grip on political affairs. Bhutto has upgraded the Women's Division to a Ministry for Women's Development, established police stations run by women, specifically to safeguard women, in Punjab and Sindh, and appointed two well-known and respected women lawyers as judges to the High Court.

A new political will?

The frequent changes of government since 1988 have hindered the planning and implementation of social reform policies, and few politicians have been committed enough to press for much-needed changes. However, since the 1993 election, many Pakistanis believe there are more hopeful signs of a firmer political will to change the status quo. Both the ruling party and the opposition Pakistan Muslim League, under Nawaz Sharif, are relatively liberal. The orthodox Jamaat-e-Islami party gained very few votes in the election. However, its leader, Qazi Hussain Ahmed, vowed to oppose family planning, charging that the government's efforts to reduce fertility are part of an "international conspiracy to reduce the Muslim population [10]".

"We have a vision of eliminating poverty, hunger and disease, and raising the quality of life of our people," says Benazir Bhutto. A newly established task force, headed by a dedicated educationist and women's activist, Shahnaz Wazir Ali, is presently analysing the existing problems in social sector development; priority is to be given to women's education and development, and family planning is to be placed within this context. This broader concept of population planning, as part of overall human development, contrasts with the previous narrow, number-oriented approach and is expected to yield positive results.

According to Nafis Sadik, UNFPA has pledged US$30 million over a five-year period from January 1994 for contraceptives, surgical sterilisations, support for non-government organisations (NGOs) and research and training. Person-to-person counselling and health care is to be provided by 12,000 village-based family planning workers and 33,000 community health workers.

This move is all the more important in view of the bombshell dropped by the United States Agency for International Development (USAID) in June 1993: because the United States disagreed with Pakistan's nuclear policies, USAID withdrew all funding for population programmes. The exact setback to government programmes has not been made public but the withdrawal of funding had an almost immediate effect. "USAID provided the major funds for population activities in Pakistan over the past several years," says Zeba Zubair, former chairperson of the NGOs' Coordinating Council for Population Affairs (NGOCC). She complains that "the human right to contraception" is being sacrificed to a political dispute. While the political situation seems to be thawing, new aid funds are not yet forthcoming.

Concern is also expressed by Said Afsheen Ahmed, of the Pakistan Voluntary Health and Nutrition Association, a large country-wide NGO: "We've built up a satisfied clientele of 100,000 and could have done even more with consistent policies and funding.... We'll lose our clients. We have only two months' supply left, and even that is less than we requisitioned."

Other reforms are underway. Thirty ordinances, including some of the Hudood Ordinances, are being re-examined by the National Assembly; and the Human Rights Commission of Pakistan has appealed for re-examination of the discriminatory *Zina* law. Further signs of the wind of change are the appointment of an eminent woman journalist, Dr Maleeha Lodhi, to the post of Ambassador to the United States, and the increase in women's seats in the National Assembly, in order to enhance their role in government.

A growing awareness

"We simply can't stop now. Woman's consciousness about herself is growing: the efforts of the various women's organisations have been catalytic," says Naheed Awan of the Lahore-based Mother and Child Welfare Association of Pakistan. "Even the Zia years of military dictatorship weren't entirely wasted.... Awareness about contraception continued to grow in that time—maybe it was dormant, but it was very much there."

Urban women tend to be more knowledgeable about contraception than their rural counterparts. Naseem, whose husband is a rickshaw driver, is waiting for contraceptive treatment at a clinic in Lahore. "My mother-in-law says children are God's gift, and their birth must not be stopped," says Naseem. "But I took the opportunity and came to the local mother and child health centre. I already have three children—two sons and a daughter. We want to send them to school—how can we do that with so much *menghai* [inflation]? So I've come for an injection."

"I've come with Naseem," chips in Ayesha, a pretty 20-year-old mother of three. "My husband insists he wants more—but there is no way.... I want an IUD put in."

"Inadequate supplies and communication spell constant setbacks," comments Sadequa Salahuddin of the Aga Khan NGO Support Programme. But, given encouragement, family planning workers are proving equal to the task, even in strongholds of conservatism. In Quetta, Baluchistan, despite the prevailing religious orthodoxy, poor transportation and insufficient supplies, Razia, a Lady Health Visitor (LHV), is very hopeful. She is project manager for the All Pakistan Women's Association family planning clinics in the region. She organises mother and child health centres and primary education classes for the children who come with their mothers, maintains records, distributes medicines, and provides counselling. "It's tough," she says. "This isn't an area where highly qualified doctors will come. We've overcome that problem, because we've built up a good referral system."

"The multi-sectoral approach is working", she continues, "but the need for basic health care is desperate and there's an immense hunger for education. Not that they're all poor, but many women are dying of puerperal sepsis [blood poisoning from infection following childbirth]. Their kids are weak. They themselves are anaemic—even little girls develop headaches because of anaemia."

Theoretically, women are free to practise almost all forms of contraception independently; only for tubal ligation is the spouse's permission necessary (not the case if a man decides to have a vasectomy).

A majority of women certainly want to exercise reproductive choice. According to a recent survey of 6,611 women, 54% of currently married women want either to postpone their next birth by at least two years, or to cease childbearing altogether. The average ideal number of children was considered to be four—in sharp contrast to the existing fertility rate of 6.3 per woman [11]. The same survey found that men are as knowledgeable as women about modern methods of family planning, and are more likely to know where to get them.

Many women wish to obtain contraception without their husbands' knowledge, fearing opposition. Euphemistically termed "shy users", they account for approximately 6% of all women using contraception, according to a recent survey by the National Institute of Population Studies [12]. This proportion is thought to be increasing.

Honour, virility...and inflation

Attitudes towards family planning are diverse, with culture and religion exerting powerful influences. "Pathans [from Baluchistan and the North West Frontier], are the least receptive to any information regarding contraception. For them, it is a matter of honour, a sign of virility, to have many children, especially sons," explains Dr Naseem Salahuddin, a Karachi-based physician who works with the poor.

"Even when they come and live in the cities, they don't permit their wives to move about independently, or seek education, or in any way alter their dress or behavioural code. The suggestion of family planning is met with severe refusal—even when the woman is ill and exhausted."

An LHV from Quetta, Baluchistan, encounters similar problems: "We aren't even allowed to enter such homes." Another LHV reports, "I managed to get into one, but the mother-in-law didn't leave me alone with the wife even for a moment. But for the last four months, I've managed to secretly get pills to her. At the same time almost every woman is afraid, because if she practises family planning, her husband may take a second wife."

Says Afsheen Ahmed of the Pakistan Voluntary Health and Nutrition Association: "Our stress is on raising awareness, bringing about attitudinal and behavioural change. We also find that most women want child spacing, they know that babies will be weak if they don't get enough attention—but it's a male and in-law dominated society: that has a significant effect on women's ability to practise family planning."

Many consider family planning to be un-Islamic. An LHV from the Quetta Regional Training Institute explains: "That is what the *maulvis* [religious leaders] say. Since they're highly respected by the villagers, we lose out. Our profession is held in contempt; we're considered corrupt and are not allowed to meet unmarried girls."

However, some family planning workers emphasise that religion is not as significant an obstacle to family planning as was once feared. Certainly, it is not only religious conservatism or lack of education which generates opposition. A doctor at a major city hospital considers contraception immoral and illegal. His colleague, speaking anonymously, recalls one incident: "He actually refused entry to a woman scheduled for a tubal ligation right at the door of the operation theatre, when the woman had already been fully masked and gowned and prepared for surgery. No action was taken against the doctor; the hospital director apparently agreed with him—and since he was the director, the matter went no further."

Begum Meher Kermani, of the All Pakistan Women's Association, asked a UN official concerned with human rights in Pakistan to comment on a woman's right to have the number of children she wants. "Are you serious?" was his dismissive reply.

For countless women, identity is intimately linked to the number of children they bear. They are afraid even to consider contraception since, if they have no more children, their husbands may well take a second wife. Most remain unaware that the Family Laws Ordinance prohibits a man's second marriage without the consent of the first wife.

"Male attitudes must change," says Naheed Awan of the Mother and Child Welfare Association of Pakistan. "We've even had husbands coming here and insisting on removal of IUDs. So, we stress male motivation—it's important to allay his, and his mother's, fears. But our efforts are small, compared to what the government could achieve. It's a learning process for us too—right now we're trying to encourage child spacing, but the majority of women still come to us after four children. We need to reach younger married women, so they can plan their families better."

"At first, we didn't get a favourable response to male motivation," says Razia, from the All Pakistan Women's Association. "We tried to put the condoms in shops as an alternative, but they ended up being sold to kids as balloons! Most of the time, it's a negative reaction to start with, but when they see we're providing health care and education for their children, attitudes change. Some even offer space for clinics."

"We find the direct approach works best," says Nighat Said Khan, director of the Behbud Association in Rawalpindi, a family planning association which believes strongly in the value of counselling "not just for the woman, but for her husband as well. We talk about the improved health of mother and child, the possibilities of seeing their children well educated, a better quality of life for husband and wife, and then discuss child spacing. It usually works. Besides, with the high cost of living..."

Dr Mohsina Bilgrami of the Chota Gharana (small family) clinic run by the Marie Stopes Society in Karachi agrees enthusiastically about the effect of simple economics. "What education and awareness-raising couldn't achieve, inflation has. I've been doing this work for the past 10 years, and I see a distinct change over the last two or three. Husbands today are far more cooperative and aware—and they're happy whether it's a girl or boy.... Our clients are from low-income groups, struggling their way up."

Mothers-in-law can also be susceptible to this argument. Ama Rasheedah in Lahore says: "My *bahu* [daughter-in-law] is also my niece. My son wanted more children—they have only one son and he wants another—but in this age of inflation, if you can bring up three children nicely, that is Allah's blessing."

Cautious optimism

Women have paid an inordinately high price for years of nationally wasted efforts, mis-spent funds, skewed priorities and lackadaisical policies. But many observers, women's rights activists and family planning workers are voicing a cautious optimism about the future.

Some are pinning their hopes on the revitalisation of the Social Action Programme (SAP) to be supported by the World Bank. This stresses female education, maternal and child health, and training and income generation for women. Family planning is to be part of an integrated programme, relying on greater coordination between the ministries of health and population.

But unease remains. "How can the public be educated when the sponsors themselves are unclear of what to do, when, where, and how? The people want results, not catchy slogans and empty words," worries Khalid Mahmood Arif [13].

In the meantime, government family planning programmes are still criticised for continuing to target women as merely passive recipients of contraception. Moreover, until such time as equitable legislation is achieved, reproductive rights are unlikely to be women's and human rights issues, a fact which troubles forward-looking groups such as the Women's Action Forum, a national feminist organisation. So far, Pakistan has not ratified the Convention for the Elimination of all Forms of Discrimination Against Women.

However, Dr Nafis Sadik senses a new dynamism and a strong political will to move forward, with Benazir Bhutto giving high priority to family planning and women's development, health, and education. What is needed, she has argued, is a virtual reconceptualisation of present population activities through reorganisation and integration with health initiatives.

"A significant problem has been the absence of stable government and consistent population policies. Pakistan needs totally new thinking—a change from its present feudal psyche. The general male attitudes are very patriarchal and condescending; there's no gender equity. Within the family, men need to reduce their authoritarian attitude and become more responsible and nurturing," states Dr Sadik. "Equally, for the population programme itself, women must have opportunities for advancement, hold key positions, be in managerial roles. We need to talk development, not just targets and quotas [14]."

One of the most significant phenomena of the past decade has been the growth of the women's movement and its effect on overall national development. Previously ignored injustices have been forced to the forefront. "What has happened", asks educationist Anita Ghulamali, "to...a country where girls and women are considered liabilities for their fathers, brothers and husbands? [Some] are depressed to...an appalling extent."

As Naheed Awan, of the Mother and Child Family Planning Association of Pakistan says, "The women's movement has been catalytic in raising women's awareness. They are now aware that they too have a right to a better quality of life, and to contraception."

The challenges are formidable, and it is the future—and perhaps lives—of the nation's young girls and women which hang in the balance.

Rites and Rights

Catholicism and contraception in Chile

By Lezak Shallat

> *Qué vamos a hacer con tantos*
> *embajadores de dioses!*
> *Me salen a cada paso*
> *con sus colmillos feroces.*
> *Apúrate, Valentina,*
> *que aumentaron los pastores*
> *porque ven que se derrumba*
> *el cuento de los sermones,*
> *¡Mamita mía!*
>
> *What are we going to do*
> *with so many divine ambassadors*
> *popping up at every step I take*
> *with their fierce fangs!*
> *Hurry, Valentina,*
> *the preachers are multiplying*
> *because they see that*
> *the fairy tale sermons*
> *are crumbling.*
> *¡Mamita mía!*

Chilean folksinger **Violeta Parra**
to Valentina Tereshkova, first woman cosmonaut

The Roman Catholic Church plays a singularly formative role in Chile, where three out of four people profess its faith, yet women are increasingly abandoning official Church teachings on childbearing and sexual and marital ethics as unsustainable in their own lives. Instead, they are making their own choices—often with the support of their clergy—in good conscience and faith. For many, contraceptive use is not an expression of selfishness, as some bishops claim, but a socially legitimate need and an indispensable tool for survival. Today, the average Chilean woman has 2.6 children, a figure that ranks amongst the lowest in Latin America (with Uruguay and Cuba).

This self-assertiveness contrasts strikingly with the Catholic fundamentalism reflected in the country's laws. Divorce is illegal, pregnant teenagers were only recently admitted into the classroom and even therapeutic abortion (abortion for medical reasons) was banned in 1989—the last in a series of measures taken by the former military government to curtail reproductive freedoms. Since the 1990 return to democracy after 17 years of military dictatorship under General Augusto Pinochet, demands for reform have met with little action from a government intent on not upsetting entrenched powers, including the Church.

Unfortunately, Church authorities—who during the military regime won national and international respect for their defence of human rights—have now turned their attention to restricting reproductive rights, censoring what they see as increasing permissiveness in society.

2,000 years of "No"

Although preached as divinely ordained and immutable, official Church teachings on sexuality, marriage and contraception have changed over the centuries.

With its affirmation that "each and every marriage act must remain open to the transmission of life", the 1968 encyclical *Humanae Vitae* codified the Roman Catholic Church's most intransigent opposition to artificial birth control. Issued by Pope Paul VI, the document rejected reforms proposed in the wake of the liberal Second Vatican Council, which had called for acceptance of artificial contraception within the framework of the Catholic doctrine on marriage.

The Vatican has also categorically opposed abortion, teaching that it is always morally wrong even when the pregnancy is the result of rape, or when there is foetal malformation. Where a mother's life is in danger the Church allows only medical measures which do not involve direct action against the life of the foetus.

The Church strongly defended human rights during Pinochet's regime but remains intransigent about reproductive rights.

Like its stance on contraception, the Church's view of abortion has not been unanimous or constant over time. Debate has centred on the question of "hominisation", the point at which the developing embryo becomes a human being with full "moral status". Ivone Gebara, a Latin American theologian, believes that abortion in the early stages of pregnancy may be permissible.

The ban on contraceptives creates a dangerous dilemma regarding abortion. By disapproving of family planning, the Church heightens the likelihood of unwanted pregnancy and increases the probability of unsafe abortion—yet it rejects legalisation as a solution.

Dissent within the Church

Humanae Vitae created dissent amongst Catholics worldwide that still persists and is evident in the widespread erosion of the Church's control over the sexual and reproductive behaviour of its followers. Polls conducted in 1993, the 25th anniversary of *Humanae Vitae*, suggest that most Catholics ignore the stricture that periodic abstinence is the only permissible form of birth control. According to one survey, 83% of 18-25 year-old Catholics in the United States believe they can disagree with church teaching and yet remain good Catholics [1].

Dissenting clergy claim there are ethical principles that could make preventive contraceptives morally acceptable in certain circumstances. They cite Church doctrines of liberty of conscience that view individual responsibility and action in the light of motivation and circumstance.

The impact of official Church doctrine is most pronounced in the South, where access to contraception and safe abortion are life and death issues for poor women. In Latin America, 40-50% of maternal deaths are caused by backstreet abortions [2].

In Chile, *Humanae Vitae* met with some praise but no great enthusiasm. "An excellent document, but it cannot be applied," said a prominent Santiago priest who saw his career sidelined for his candour. Fear of discipline helps explain the contradictory posture that prevails today: from the pulpit, many priests reject contraceptive use; in the confessional, they counsel parishioners to follow their conscience.

"The Church believes in responsible maternity-paternity, in couples having the number of children that they can take care of," explains Father Antonio Mifsud, a Jesuit educator and advisor to the government's 1991 Consultative Commission on Sex Education. "The decision is the couple's. Our moral function is to pose ideals and look at reality. After that, we must have faith in the people."

It is at the grassroots that clergy, nuns and laity—many of them inspired by the Liberation Theology movement of the 1960s that called for social action in defence of the poor—are most often to be found dispensing modern contraceptives in community clinics, in contravention of Vatican rulings but in accordance with their consciences. Some draw the line at IUDs, which they reject as abortifacients, but others accept this method. A nun in a rural clinic in southern Chile tells family planning officials how proud she is to have inserted her 500th IUD: "For women, I am a midwife. For the Church, I am a nun who fulfils the dictates of her conscience."

Midwife Despina Bongiorno, a practising Catholic, is adamant: "I would never go against family planning. How could I tell a woman who lives in a slum with her three children that she shouldn't use birth control methods for religious reasons?... We must try to avoid the birth of children who are unwanted. The love that my Church preaches is the love that I pass on through my care, so they won't have septic abortions and children they cannot support."

In October 1993—25 years after *Humanae Vitae*—Pope John Paul II released the encyclical *Veritatis Splendor*, partly to silence dissenting voices by reiterating traditional Catholic Church teaching on moral absolutes based on natural law: abortion is wrong and every artificial contraceptive act is "intrinsically evil". Even the global spread of HIV/AIDS has failed to modify the Vatican's stance against condoms, a contraceptive that also reduces transmission of this incurable disease.

Underlying the official doctrines on sexual practices is the hierarchy's teaching on authority. The document takes a hard line on papal authority, instructing theologians to accept rather than interpret.

"Contraceptive imperialism"

Many Southern commentators have voiced concern that Northern governments and agencies are intent on reducing the number of Third World children rather than campaigning for debt forgiveness and an equitable distribution of wealth. This argument is now being aired by Chilean clergy as well.

Monsignor Cristián Caro, general secretary of the 1993 Chilean Bishops' Conference, opened the session by challenging those who see contraception as the solution to the problems of poverty and hunger in the world. "The Church firmly states that the solution to these problems is not a question of limiting births", he insisted, "but of producing more resources and distributing them better, because these problems are caused by selfishness and the misuse and maldistribution of production [3]."

Similarly, Santiago priest Raúl Hasbún recently used his weekly newspaper column to denounce the "demographic terrorism" in Latin America and the Caribbean that "exaggerates the danger posed by population growth to the quality of life". He continued: "Our continent suffers from 'contraceptive imperialism' that consists of imposing on peoples and cultures all forms of contraception, sterilisation and abortion [4]."

Feminists, in particular, are uncomfortable at hearing their arguments voiced by the Church in the context of attempts to restrict all access to modern contraceptives. Although both camps reject coercion, experimentation and manipulation of women's dignity, the Catholic Church does not accept women's individual right to self determination, including the right to reproductive choice. On the contrary, it rejects human intervention in the life-and-death questions it views as divine territory.

"Church doctrine clearly states that all artificial contraception is objectively evil and cannot be an ethical choice," writes Frances Kissling, president of Catholics for a Free Choice, a pro-choice movement with offices in the United States and Latin America. "Women's groups and family planning advocates believe that the human right to choice on the basis of personal values is overridden by this absolute prohibition."

She asserts that the Church fears that open discussion of population issues could lead to more widespread acceptance of the family planning methods it condemns. "This attitude limits its capacity to participate in the population debate; sadly so, since the Church's emphasis on human rights and social justice, and its vision of the world as an interdependent instead of a competitive society, could amplify the voices of those seeking to place population policies in a moral context [5]."

Other critics take a harsher view. "The 'masculine Church' has always condemned women's bodies," writes Brazilian theologian Ivone Gebara. "It has never interested itself in women's problems, in the tragic living situations that society imposes [6]."

Updating the morality crusade

The Chilean Church's defence of human rights during the dictatorship earned it respect and moral authority, a legacy that has allowed it to address society on moral issues with a heightened sense of legitimacy.

Upper-class ideological movements such as Schoenstatt and Opus Dei, comparable to the Moral Majority in the United States, have grown in number and influence in Chile. Opus Dei runs a university and numerous schools and has a powerful influence over the mass media. In 1993 the Vatican granted Chile its first saint, Teresa de los Andes, a cloistered nun whose short and prayerful life is revered as a model for Chilean youth. In the same year, the Santiago archbishop's office closed its world-renowned human rights office, the *Vicaria de la Solidaridad*.

Nowadays, bishops have little to say about politics or the economy but are increasingly vocal in their public declarations on sexual morality. The final session of the 1993 Chilean Bishops' Conference was devoted to analysing the "threats" facing the Chilean family. Unimpressed by polls showing 74% of Chileans in favour of legal divorce, Monsignor Caro argued: "If 76.7% of the population say they are Catholic, the Church's position on this matter cannot be ignored [7]."

The Church is restating old messages but has modernised its language. It is tapping into the uncertainties felt by many at the end of this century. According to Sister Verónica Morandé, executive secretary of the National Family Pastoral Commission, the Roman Catholic faith offers a haven from today's "throw-away" culture, with its godless belief in science and technology and its rampant consumerism: "This is the age of disposable relations—'I take you, I use you, I dump you'—between men and women. These attitudes undermine values of fidelity and admiration, and reward individualism based on competition, not solidarity."

Talk about sex is no longer taboo: Church outreach programmes offer guidance on marriage and couple relationships, and information on natural birth control. Nor are "sinners" cast aside: there are Church-run maternity homes, and support groups for single mothers and separated spouses. In 1994, the Bishops' Conference opened a new Family Institute to improve counselling skills and influence public opinion. Catholic schools, which make up the majority of private schools in the country, have jumped into the sex education fray with comprehensive programmes to impart "Education for Love and Sexuality" [8].

Many Catholics are disquieted by the widening gap they see between the Church's official discourse and the reality of family life: between the Holy Family and the Chilean one. One liberal Catholic who works with the Church charges it with taking an apocalyptic view of this chasm and failing to examine its socio-economic causes. "The real crime in this country where one-third of the people live in poverty is the failure to provide the minimum conditions and support that would stop abortion," he adds.

As Francisco López, head of the social sciences faculty at the Jesuit school ILADES, noted in a Catholic newsletter on Latin America: "The underlying problem is that the Chilean Church is not really prepared to deal with the modern world, and Chile is modernising very rapidly [9]."

Democracy or theocracy?

Chile's family law is surprisingly conservative. Divorce is outlawed and adultery is technically a punishable offence, with more lenient definitions and sanctions for men than women. There is official discrimination—regarding inheritance and paternal support—against illegitimate children (one-third of all births in 1990), who also cannot join the Armed Forces or enter many parochial schools [10].

One feature of Chile's new political system is the alliance between the government and the Catholic Church. "In Chile, the Church influences governments, not women," says Dr Benjamin Viel, a founder of the Chilean family planning association APROFA.

The government, led by the Christian Democrats, was quick to create the nation's first Ministry for Women but has failed to effect reforms that would improve women's lives. Legislation stymied by Congress includes proposals on divorce, therapeutic abortion, domestic violence, sexual harassment and discrimination against illegitimate children. Legal progress is also hampered by the major media, which are highly influenced by groups such as Opus Dei. According to former Socialist congressman Dr Carlos Smok, the media have created "the divor-bortion monster" and inhibit debate on a diverse range of family and reproductive health issues.

Dr Smok is still shocked by the brutal reaction that greeted his 1991 effort to reinstate therapeutic abortion. One bishop threatened to excommunicate any legislator approving the measure—a threat that affects half of Congress.

But mobilising for abortion reform is also hampered by the lingering reluctance of human rights and public health activists to oppose a Church that stood by them throughout the dictatorship. Psychologist Miren Asunción Busto is angry about the little that has been accomplished in five years of democracy but she admits: "I am afraid to tell the Church what I feel. I owe a lot to the Church."

An example of political compromise at the expense of responsible health policy is the Ministry of Education's new sex education project. Recent studies show that the average Chilean youth first has sexual intercourse between the ages of 16 and 17 [11], and each year some 40,000 teenage girls have babies [12]. But, under attack from the religious right for promoting a "condom culture", and after considerable debate, education officials beat a retreat and issued a decree leaving responsibility for sex education programmes to municipal officials. The result: many public schools turn a blind eye to reality and fail to inform their students about modern contraception and the importance of "safe sex".

Abortion: changes and reversals

Therapeutic abortion was legalised in the 1930s. But as infant mortality rates dropped and family size grew without corresponding increases in income, by the 1950s more and more women were turning to backstreet abortionists for economic and psychological reasons. By 1965, hospital obstetric services were emptying beds in order to free them for septic abortion cases. Studies conducted during the 1960s suggest some 80% of these abortions were performed on adult married women with several children, indicating that abortion was principally used to limit family size rather than "hide" pre-marital relations [13].

In the mid-1960s, pro-contraceptive campaigns launched by feminists 30 years earlier were taken up by doctors, who argued that abortions were not being stopped by Catholic religious teachings or by punitive penal codes, under which women seeking illegal abortions and those performing them risked going to jail. As a result of these campaigns a policy of abortion prevention using modern contraceptives was approved in 1965 by a Christian Democratic administration. It authorised the national health service to provide Chilean women with free contraceptives donated by the United States Agency for International Development (USAID) and other international agencies. Although pro-life groups objected, the programme grew steadily over the next decade.

The military regime that came to power in 1973 reversed this trend. Guided by its in-house Catholic ideologues, the regime granted concessions to the Church in the area of reproductive health to mollify priestly wrath over the abuse of human rights. In 1978, with the adoption by the military government of a pro-natalist policy that cited "national security" reasons for stimulating population growth, the programme of birth control information in community clinics was suspended and the provision of contraceptives limited to cases of "spontaneous demand"; some women had IUDs removed during gynaecological examinations without having given informed consent. The regime's final blow, however, was its 1989 ban on therapeutic abortion, justified—it claimed—on the grounds that high standards of health care in Chile eliminated any need for abortion for medical reasons.

Therapeutic abortions represent a tiny fraction of the total number of abortions performed every year—estimated as 150,000-175,000 [14], and roughly equivalent to one abortion for every two live births [15].

Many Chilean women believe they can act according to their conscience on contraception and remain good Catholics.

With increases in contraceptive use, the profile of the woman who turns to abortion has changed. No longer is she usually married with children. According to a recent study of 400 women hospitalised for incomplete abortion, more than half were single. A growing percentage of women are under the age of 20 and not living with their partners [16].

Women who obtain an illegal abortion have to contend with many fears—of health risks, of criminal conviction (since they are occasionally denounced, sometimes by their own doctors) and of divine punishment. But attitudes are changing. Studies show that women's personal experiences and those of relatives and friends have overridden legal and religious prohibitions. A 1992 Santiago poll found that more than 70% of respondents approved of abortion for medical reasons; more than 50% approved in cases of rape; and nearly 20% held that abortion is permissible for socio-economic reasons or because the woman requests it [17].

A woman's decision to end a pregnancy rarely comes easily. Although she may have strong religious misgivings, she may still feel forced by circumstances to seek an abortion. "I know it is a sin, but God will understand me," is a common feeling. As Dr Cristina Grela, of the Latin American chapter of Catholics for a Free Choice, notes: "When we choose, at a given moment in our lives, to have an abortion in good conscience, believing it to be the best step for us at that time, we are still Catholics."

Psychologists who have worked with Catholic women after abortion note that although many feel remorse, they still feel Catholic. Some even consider the distress they feel a necessary penance. But despite conflicts, many women feel an overriding sense of relief. Three studies conducted in Chilean hospitals revealed that despite the difficulties and dangers involved in the abortion process, many women close this chapter of their lives with a strong sense of relief at having done the right thing [18].

Chile's annual population growth rate has fallen from 2.5% in 1965 to 1.7% in 1994, and many experts suspect the government of having an unacknowledged population policy that relies on abortion as a contraceptive method. Not only does this policy expose women to dangerous health risks, critics charge; it hypocritically avoids confrontation with the Church by utilising abortion without approving it. However, lack of information—the military regime refused to conduct the last scheduled fertility survey—makes it hard to confirm this theory or to form an up-to-date picture of contraception use. A 1989 survey by APROFA of women of child-bearing age in the Santiago metropolitan area indicated that 55.6% use contraceptives regularly.

Machismo and Marianismo

Male chauvinism is so closely associated with Latin American culture that *machismo*, the Spanish word for these attitudes, has crossed linguistic borders. *Machismo* operates on many levels, including the law, which allows men the option of choosing whether or not to recognise a child born out of wedlock.

For many a Latin American *macho*, children are a sign of virility. This is one of the reasons a man might send his wife back to the doctor to have her IUD removed—if, in fact, she has the courage to tell him she has had one inserted. Another is that although he feels free to have extra-marital sexual relations, he does not want freedom from pregnancy to give her similar ideas.

Machismo has its female counterpart in *Marianismo*: ideals embodied in the Catholic devotion to Mary, virgin and mother, paragon of chastity, meekness and submission. *Marianismo* glorifies motherhood and denies women's sexuality, and is so pervasive that women who chose not to bear children are often viewed as selfish, frivolous and unnatural.

In this culture, Chilean women's ability to carry out autonomous decisions about reproductive matters is often more illusory than real. In 1988, Chilean sociologist Teresa Valdés conducted an in-depth study of childbearing decisions among poor women in Santiago. Of 26 women interviewed, only three had planned their first pregnancy; and of the 97 children born to these women, the great majority—61—were also unplanned [19].

Inadequate government public health and family planning services are further factors underlying the numbers of unplanned pregnancies. Women need great determination in the face of long waiting lists, unexplained delays, lack of information and authoritarian doctor-patient relationships. Or they may be unable to attend the clinic for lack of bus fare, babysitter or time-off from work.

Motherhood may also be a statement in the face of limited options. For many Chileans, the dictatorship and the imposition of economic "shock treatment" swept away cherished dreams. Teresa Valdés explains: "Everything came to a halt.... In this state of affairs, when everything crumbles, the security of nature—immutable and permanent—reappears with force in the prospect of motherhood.... It's no longer a matter of having more children for more help with family sustenance. It's a matter of giving meaning to life in an exclusionary culture [20]."

The challenge of the new

Just two generations ago, most Chilean women never imagined that they could safely and reliably control their fertility. Today, many of their daughters and granddaughters view birth control as a right.

Rosa Zerega, a nurse at the University of Tarapacá medical service, provides contraceptives to university students, married or not, who do not want their studies interrupted. "The girls come looking for safety," she says. "They have a tremendous thirst for information. They ask questions. They make demands. And they don't get up from their chairs until I give them answers."

Not long ago, Carmen and Andrés Poblete (not their real names), who already had eight children, stopped going to confession when they started using condoms. However, Catholic women today are just as likely to echo the words of Marianela González, a former catechism teacher: "I've been freeing myself of the fears that the Church instilled in me. The priests have no right to direct my sexuality. We are all the Church."

Marianela is not alone in being a feminist Catholic who nevertheless still has difficulties with the issue of abortion: "I still have ghosts," she confesses. "Abortion is still a taboo. I am certain that it is women who must choose, but I feel lost at sea. Why do we feel guilt? Could it be that we feel afraid when we leave the narrow path we were taught to follow?"

A growing number of Catholic women are advocating a new relationship with the Church. Spirituality collectives such as Conspirando explore issues of sexuality and authority, abortion and AIDS. On the regional level, the Latin American branch of Catholics for a Free Choice—Católicas por el Derecho a Decidir—promotes dialogue with clergy, legislators and legal and health professionals, while providing its grassroots constituency with a steady stream of publications. But despite its international profile, Católicas has found it hard to gain an organisational foothold in Chile because of the reluctance of activists there to openly oppose the Church.

Losing the women

The Roman Catholic Church lost a good number of its intellectuals and scientists in the eighteenth century; in the nineteenth century it lost the workers, and now it is losing women, writes Uruguayan priest Luis Pérez Aguirre, in his 1993 book *La Iglesia Increíble* (The Incredible Church). The author, a Jesuit, has been silenced pending examination of the book by the Uruguayan Bishops' Conference, but his conclusion cannot be so easily dismissed.

As the twentieth century draws to a close, advances in reproductive technology are forcing individuals and societies to confront a minefield of bio-ethical dilemmas. In Chile, for example, new pre-natal diagnostic technologies are being evaluated in view of the increased impact of environmental hazards such as pesticides on foetal development—an issue which cannot be divorced from that of therapeutic abortion.

Chileans will eventually have to grapple with technologies such as the RU486 "abortion pill", which blurs distinctions between contraceptives and abortifacients. Nor will they be able to ignore experiments using genetic engineering and foetal tissue, and developments in eugenics, euthanasia and organ transplants, each with its ethical questions and scientific-commercial context.

The Chilean Catholic Church could offer women and men relevant moral guidance to keep pace with these dizzying technological developments, but until it takes into account the most basic need to have reproductive choice and health, few Chilean women will still be listening.

In this fundamental area of human rights, change is inevitable although the pace is slow. "We have made progress in influencing culture, in questioning gender roles," says Dr Maria Isabel Matamala, of Chile's Open Forum on Reproductive Health and Rights. "The subjects that people are talking about are our subjects. Sexuality has become a political issue."

In the Shadow of a Man

Social forces and women's rights in Egypt

By Dina Ezzat

Talking excitedly, a crowd of high school girls pours into the already packed women's compartment of the metro train heading for one of Alexandria's poorer districts. The topic of their conversation: the "beautiful news" of the recent engagement of a school mate.

"She seems very happy. I am sure her mother is happy too...."

Only the jolting stops and starts of the train at stations along the route briefly interrupt the conversation. From time to time the girls wearing headscarves—by far the majority of the group—adjust them a little if they slip with the lurching of the train. Everyone has something to say about the prospects of her engaged friend. For 45 minutes the subject does not change.

In Egypt, this is not an exceptional reaction. Only a birth announcement can stimulate more happiness than the news of a girl's engagement or wedding. Whether she belongs to the Muslim majority or the Christian minority, to the small rich class or the vast poor one, a typical Egyptian girl sees her future as marriage and children.

A woman's place

Although school enrolment for Egyptian girls is still only around 40%, of those who do go to school an increasing proportion go on to college and gain professional qualifications. However, even for many educated women, the first priority is home, husband and children. Women have served in the Egyptian cabinet for over two decades, but even a minister is subject to her husband's will: a few years ago Aisha Ratib, then Minister of Social Affairs, was prevented by her husband from flying to an international conference. Egyptian personal status laws still require the husband's written authorisation before a woman can be issued with a passport.

Egyptian society is typically uncomfortable with the idea of women acting on their own initiative and believes they need male protectors. Its attitude is evident in the popular saying, "Better the shadow of a man than the shadow of a wall": a woman is always in the shadow, and the shadow of a husband is preferable to that of loneliness.

Living alone as a single woman is virtually impossible, yet an Egyptian woman is marriageable only if she observes strict rules, of which the first and most important is chastity.

The virginity code

Preserving virginity underlies the practice of *khitan*—female "circumcision", or genital mutilation—to which an estimated 70% or more of Egyptian girls are subjected [1]. This operation entails the partial or total removal of the clitoris and—in some cases of the *labia minora* and even the *labia majora*. Older female relatives hold the girl's arms and legs down while the *daya* (midwife) cuts into her genitalia with a knife or razor. After the operation, considered to mark the transition to womanhood, female relatives ululate to express their happiness, while the girl is served with special meals and given small sums of money and other gifts. *Khitan* signals her readiness for marriage.

By removing the part of her body that gives her sexual pleasure, society believes it controls women's sexuality. The husband's "needs" and enjoyment are seen as paramount.

Sociologist Dr Marie Asaad says virginity is usually equated with an unbroken hymen and that a typical Egyptian man would be furious if his wife did not bleed on her wedding night, thus proving her chastity. In rural Egypt, he could divorce her the following morning, publicly revealing her shame and dishonour.

Many Egyptians do not know that the hymen can stretch or break from everyday activities such as riding on the back of an animal, or that on defloration a flexible hymen does not bleed, says Aziza Kamil, chairperson of the Cairo-based Association for Combating Unhealthy Practices, which works to eliminate excision. Even when told these facts people may refuse to believe them as they lack even basic knowledge about the reproductive systems of men and women.

Dukhla baladi (finger defloration) is one traditional test of chastity. On the morning of a woman's wedding, a *daya* (an older female relative) uses her finger to pierce the bride's hymen. The "blood of honour" is taken on a white handkerchief and shown to the groom and his relatives who have been waiting in an adjacent room, and then to neighbours and friends waiting outside. The bride's father and the groom then accept felicitations. According to Dr Asaad, this practice—though less common than female genital mutilation—is relatively widespread and is even carried out in parts of the major cities such as Cairo and Alexandria.

Both practices entail risks to women's health. In the case of severe forms of genital mutilation, there may be excessive bleeding which, if not treated immediately, can leave the girl dreadfully weak or may even kill her. Substandard hygiene often leads to serious infections and scarring. Finger defloration, if improperly performed, can damage the women's uterus or bladder. Both practices cause immediate and long-term psychological suffering.

Society enforces these practices to gain control over women's bodies, says psychiatrist and leading Egyptian feminist Dr Nawal Al-Saadawi. "And it has trained women even to look forward to this physical and psychological pain."

Hind Khattab, author of the *The Silent Endurance* which describes women's stoicism in the face of health problems, explains that society teaches young women to endure such practices and even the treatable pains of menstruation as part of the experience of becoming a wife and a mother. Adolescent girls are often told by their mothers not to complain about menstruation pains as these are "signs of fertility [2]".

Population policy and women's health

Women's health and reproductive rights and choices came into the limelight in Egypt only recently. The trigger was birth control.

In the early 1960s the government began to realise that it had too few resources to meet the needs of a rapidly growing population, already numbering 26 million. It therefore launched a national family planning programme which was extended in the mid-1970s. The government programme, according to Aziza Hussein, chairperson of the Cairo Family Planning Association, was set up primarily with demographic goals, whereas some earlier programmes run by non-government organisations (NGOs) had aimed to improve women's overall health. Today, critics say, the approach of many NGOs is hardly distinguishable from that of government.

The government at first talked about its programme as a "birth control campaign", says psychiatrist Aida Seif Al-Dawla, a member of New Woman Association, a newly formed feminist NGO. Later, realising that this emphasis was unpopular, it adopted the term "family planning". Ideally, Dr Seif Al-Dawla remarks, this means that married couples make well-founded reproductive choices.

Today, the family planning programme has over 3,000 clinics nationwide. These are meant to provide comprehensive gynaecological care, especially to rural women who for years have lacked access to contraceptives and have had to depend on poorly trained midwives for help during pregnancy and birth.

"We are launching a state-wide programme to upgrade the standard of services provided by hundreds of midwives," promises Maher Mahran, Minister of Population and Family Welfare. "We believe that midwives are an integral part of the system of rural health services and we want to make the best use of them."

Officials maintain that great changes have occurred over the last 40 years and that most women now have access to proper medical help. They cite the increase in contraceptive use by married couples from 10% in the 1960s to 50% today as evidence of success and emphasise that birth spacing has helped women cope better with the heavy demands on them.

"The Egyptian government is aware of all the problems of women," claims Maher Mahran. "We know that Egyptian women work harder than men, they carry all the load of housework, assist their husbands in the field and when they get pregnant they must continue to do so." More recently, the ministry of health has developed plans to include user satisfaction in the criteria for assessing the performance of family planning services.

"Good health care is not that accessible to rural and poorer women," asserts Dr Seif Al-Dawla. However, according to Dr Laila Nawar, a senior demographer with the Population Council's regional office for the Middle East, there is a family planning unit no more than 5 km from nearly every Egyptian family. The problem, according to critics, is that these units are more often preoccupied with distributing contraceptives than providing health care.

Contraceptive options are also restricted, say critics of the national programme. Some 60% of women using contraception have had

IUDs fitted, according to the Ministry of Population and Welfare [3]. An official working on the national programme, speaking anonymously, concedes: "It is true that some clinics have a very limited choice of contraceptives, but that is because they have to make do with whatever they receive from the international organisations supporting them."

"There is no choice at all in telling a woman that she can either keep giving birth to more children or use a contraceptive she is not comfortable with," Dr Seif Al-Dawla argues. But the Minister of Population and Family Welfare insists: "All family planning clinics provide a cafeteria-style service."

The attitude of health providers in family planning clinics is also questioned. Sudanese physician Nahid Tubia, of the Population Council in New York, says doctors talk down to women. Dr Seif Al-Dawla says doctors "prescribe" methods rather than discussing alternatives with recipients. "They want the woman to use the IUD because they do not trust her long-term cooperation," she adds.

"The doctor said the IUD is best for me because I am young and would not remember to take the Pill on time," says Dalia, a 25-year-old university graduate quoting her expensive gynaecologist.

Azza, a primary school drop-out from a rural area recalls: "The doctor said he would insert it for me and I would forget all about it for the coming five years after which I would go to him to remove it and put in a new one."

"Doctors want to be in control," Dr Tubia says. "They want to be the ones to insert and the ones to remove it." Doctors are also accused of failing to inform women about possible side effects.

According to Nawal Al-Saadawi, who has long opposed the way in which family planning programmes in developing countries are run, clinics do not treat women as human beings with minds and wills of their own. She claims that the national programme "takes the authority from the hands of the husband and puts it in the hands of government....If the government cared about women it would have spent the money on improving women's health and status."

Myths and self-sacrifice

Dr Al-Saadawi says the family planning programme has failed to extend health information to women, which is crucial if their health and lives are to improve. Instead, misinformation abounds. "A woman feeling regular minor pain during intercourse or noticing unusual vaginal secretion will not get a check-up because she would think it is an unalarming thing," says Hayam Salah Al-Din, a gynaecologist. Recent research in a district south of Cairo found low-income rural women suffer an extreme burden of reproductive health problems: of more than 500 women, half had reproductive tract infections and more than half had genital prolapse [4].

Myths about contraceptives are widespread. "I would not use the IUD," says Zena, a 30-year-old illiterate rural woman. "A friend of mine used it and it moved out of her womb, pierced her heart and came out of her ear."

Male contraceptive use is minimal since Egyptian society views birth control as the responsibility of women, an attitude reinforced by media commercials promoting female contraceptives. According to Sawsan Al-Sheikh, who runs a family planning clinic, most men refuse to use a condom because they say it prevents them from enjoying sex or is "degrading to their masculinity". Many women agree—"No, no, no. What are you talking about? A man wearing a condom!" exclaims one group—but they often have difficulty gaining their husbands' permission to use contraceptives themselves.

"I had my first baby two years ago and I did not want to get pregnant again for two or three years," says Nawal, a 26-year-old semi-literate woman living in the city. After long arguments with her husband, she gave up. Only after the birth of a second baby did he capitulate, but even then he would not let her use an IUD because of misinformation from his friends at work. "One colleague whose wife had an IUD told me that it would tighten around me when I get inside my wife," he says.

Nor did he want her to use the Pill. "My sister used it and she kept looking thinner no matter what she ate." Eventually he agreed to Nawal having quarterly hormone injections (Depo Provera).

Men's intransigence and lack of knowledge forces some women to use contraceptives clandestinely, normally choosing methods such as the Pill or Depo Provera which the husband will not detect. And many women, out of a combination of self-sacrifice and lack of knowledge, and because of the inaccessibility of care, do not look after their physical wellbeing. Unless their performance as wives and mothers is handicapped, says Hind Khattab, they do not complain about symptoms of illness.

"We are living in a society where everything is based on how the man feels about this, that or the other," says gynaecologist Salah Al-Din. "A wife cannot do or suggest anything that will annoy her husband. Even if her health is at risk she still has to tolerate it."

One of Dr Salah Al-Din's patients suffered from a recurrent vaginal infection transmitted by her husband who was unwilling to undergo medical treatment. The patient could neither force her husband to see a doctor nor convince him to use a condom. Dr Salah Al-Din says that women know very little, if anything, about sexually transmitted diseases—a subject which is ignored by schools and the media.

Aziza, a 26-year-old househelp, provides for her two children as well as her husband, who refuses to take a job but appropriates most of her pay to spend on drinking and gambling. Aziza suffered from severe kidney pain for several months but was unable to go to the doctor because her husband left her no money.

"Only when I fell on the floor screaming did the neighbours take me to the doctor," she says. Treatment entailed two months away from her children, whom she had to send to her sister because her husband would not provide for them while she was off work.

The cultural norm that requires women to tolerate without complaint any pain related to their reproductive functions costs some women their lives. Maher Mahran says that the current maternal mortality rate in Egypt is quite high: of every 100,000 pregnant women, 200 die before or during childbirth. In most cases, death is due to causes that could easily have been diagnosed and treated. Sometimes mismanagement of labour by unqualified or poorly trained birth attendants is to blame.

Early marriages and pregnancies account for some deaths, says Sawsan Al-Sheikh, director of a family planning clinic in Alexandria. Rural parents favour early marriages for girls, the theory being that they prevent girls from "falling into sin". The minimum legal age for marriage for women is 16 but the law is not strictly applied. As many as 25% of all marriages may be under age, according to the research centre of the New Woman Association. Sometimes girls as young as 10 marry and conceive before their reproductive systems are ready to handle the burden of pregnancy. Sociologists argue that so long as society believes a woman's primary role is to marry and give birth to children it will turn a blind eye to age violations.

When a couple fails to have a child within their first year of marriage, accusations are often directed against the woman. In many cases men refuse to have their "manhood" questioned, and women are often reluctant to ask their husbands to take fertility tests. Dr Salah Al-Din recalls: "Once a female patient had to run to the clinic less than two hours after having intercourse so that we could take a sample of her husband's sperm for the test."

Even the decision to limit family size is rarely straightforward. Many women believe they need to have lots of children—and they have a point, says Dr Seif Al-Dawla. High infant mortality rates mean that a woman can lose many of her offspring. Besides, in traditional society, children act as a buffer against poverty, as they start work young, and provide company and care in old age, as well as tying a woman's husband to her.

"Bringing the son"

Egyptian women have an additional reproductive responsibility: bearing a son. Men want a son to carry on their name and both parents look to a son for support when they are old. In rural Egypt, a woman unable to "bring the son" is dispensable. For the sake of having a son a man may use his legal right to repudiate his wife or to take an additional wife.

The belief is that a woman's marriage is more secure if she bears him a son, says sociologist Dr Marie Asaad, but adds that for women there are more reasons for wanting a boy than that of satisfying their husbands' wishes. Traditionally, when all the daughters have married and moved away, it is a son who brings his wife to live in his parents' house, help his mother and take care of the housework. Few older women can afford either a househelp or labour-saving machines, and the assistance of a younger relative is invaluable.

Moreover, an only son receives half of his dead father's estate, from which he normally provides for his mother and sisters, who share the remaining half with other relatives. If there is more than one son they divide this inheritance between them. A woman can only ever inherit half as much as each son. If there is no son, Egyptian inheritance law allows much of the estate to go to the father's brothers and, in some cases, even to uncles and male cousins.

Soha, a 20-year-old rural woman, and her husband Farag were disappointed that their first newborn was a girl. Soha wanted a boy "to please Farag" and so that there would be someone to look after her if anything happened to her husband. "My father died and so will my uncles and I have no brothers.... We also need a son to accept condolences when we die." Egyptians place great importance in the ceremony held after a funeral, where a male relative—preferably a son—accepts condolences on behalf of the whole family.

Qadria is a 58-year-old civil servant and the mother of three girls and a boy. She says she loves her children equally, but has always treated her son Hossam "in a special way": "I have always appreciated him and taught his sisters to love and respect him." A 30-year-old engineer, Hossam is entitled to the best view of the television and is waited on by either his mother or one of his sisters, all of whom go out to work. When he comes into the living room his mother will always tell one of the daughters "Stand up and give your chair to your brother." "We were brought up to know that it is our duty to respect and comfort our brother," they explain.

The religion debate

Islam is the religion of over 90% of the Egyptian population, according to the last national census in 1993. Shariaa, Islam's civil law, is also the primary source of Egyptian law. For instance, Egyptian law, in accordance with the prevailing Shariaa interpretation on the matter, prohibits abortion except in very limited circumstances: when there is a threat to the mother's life or health, or in cases of certain foetal malformations.

According to Egypt's supreme religious authority, the Grand Mufti Dr Mohamed Tantawi, abortion is permissible when pregnancy constitutes a serious threat to the mother's health, but must be carried out in the first trimester, before the "ensoulment" of the foetus. He points out that Islam does not deny the woman who wants to plan her family the right to seek a suitable and reliable contraceptive. Islamic religious authorities elsewhere extend the legitimacy of abortion to cases where the babies would be born with a deformity or fatal disease and even to unwanted pregnancies.

The application of religious rulings in Egypt denies women the right to choose abortion, say feminists favouring secular laws. They argue that since no contraceptive method is 100% effective and since contraceptive services are inadequate, safe early abortion should be an option open to women. In its absence, women with unwanted pregnancies resort to using untrained birth attendants, female friends or relatives, or attempt to terminate pregnancies themselves.

Shariaa is also held responsible by its critics for marital insecurity. As interpreted in Egyptian law, it gives men licence to pursue divorce by decree alone or to take up to four wives. This drives many women to disregard their own wishes and abide by their husbands' will, believes Amira Sonbol, professor of Egyptian history at Georgetown University, Washington DC. But Islamic scholars maintain that Islam allows divorce only in cases where the couple cannot tolerate living together, and allows polygamy only if absolutely necessary for health or social reasons.

But many men think their rights are absolute. Mohamed Al-Hashash, a 68-year-old owner of a small taxi service, says he had three wives at the same time because he "wanted to stay in a good mood". In his words: "Women are like fruits. A banana has no right to tell the eater not to eat an apple if he wants." His 34-year-old son Ahmed, a taxi driver, has one wife. He would have taken another but says: "Providing for even one is hard enough nowadays—and thank God I have a boy and a girl."

According to Afaf Mahfouz, a former professor of law at Helwan University, Islam does not sanction control over women by men and should not be blamed for some Muslims' abuses: "Shariaa is a scapegoat of a society that interprets it in the way that subdues women."

Ma'moun Al-Hodeibi, spokesperson for the fundamentalist Islamic group, the Muslim Brotherhood, asserts that Shariaa grants women the right to financial independence—the essence of decision making. Islam is not responsible for the socially inherited beliefs that women are subordinate to men, Hodeibi says, and regards men and women as equal. "Islam only gave the man the right to lead the household since he is more rational than the woman, who is known to be too emotional," he adds.

The Muslim Brotherhood and other radical Islamic groups are held responsible by the Egyptian women's movement for undermining women's status in Egypt, and depriving them of their freedom and rights. "Their argument is that it is more honourable for a woman to stay at home", says Seif Al-Dawla, "and that a woman's job degrades her rather than giving her status."

Many women seem to go along with this. "A woman should stay at home because when she goes out she has to put up with harassment," says Samiha, a law student who is veiled from head to toe. After graduating she intends to stay at home.

Over the last decade, thousands of Muslim women have taken to wearing the veil or headscarf in line with the dress code prescribed by many Egyptian Islamic scholars, which allows women to show only their face and hands. Others have gone further and wear veils which reveal only their eyes.

Radical Islamic groups began to gain a hold in the late 1970s when they accused both government and society as a whole of corruption, caused by deviation from the Islamic path. Their call for a return to the true Islam was welcomed by large numbers of people frustrated by the failure of the socialist regime that ended in the early 1970s, who saw it as offering a potential way out of the economic crisis and a unifying force in the face of Israeli control of the occupied territories.

With the continuing economic crisis and political setbacks, the influence and popularity of the radical Islamic movement has expanded even further. "But so far those groups have spoken about nothing except what women should and shouldn't do," says Nawal Al-Saadawi. "So far they have been obsessed only with covering a woman's body and making sure she stays at home."

"It is God's command that women cover their bodies," says Ma'moun Al-Hodeibi. "And we are not opposed to women's work, but her first responsibility is her home. And a working woman has to take a job suitable to her fragile nature and consistent with her duties as mother and a wife." Teaching children and nursing are the examples he cites. Feminists describe this argument as reactionary and point to a deterioration in the situation of women in recent decades.

One step forward, two steps back

In the 1960s primary education was made compulsory for girls as well as boys. During this decade some women went to university, aiming for professional employment and an independent status in society.

"The movies of that era portrayed women as strong-willed personalities who chose their future and their lives," says Seif Al-Dawla. "But today's movies give an image of a woman who is either a floozie or religious."

Jehan Sadat, Egypt's former first lady, agrees about the gains for women in the 1960s and early 1970s. "They all benefited from the compulsory education law and they all benefited from the amended Personal Status Law," she says.

As first lady, she had campaigned to change some of the harshest and most discriminatory aspects of the Personal Status Law. The amended law, unprecedentedly, gave a woman the right to keep the marital home if her husband divorced her while she still had custody of young children. It also raised the age up to which a mother has custody of her children to 12 for girls and nine for boys, and allowed the judge to extend her custody to 15 for a son and until marriage for a daughter. Previously, upon divorce and in the absence of a judge's extension, a woman automatically lost custody of any daughters aged eight or above and any sons aged seven or above. The new law obliged every man to inform his wife of a second marriage and to grant her a

Three generations: will young Egyptian women regain the ground lost over more than two decades?

divorce if she did not accept his polygamy within one year.

"Jehan's Law", as it came to be known, met with severe opposition from the religious establishment. Sadat accuses those who opposed the amendments of being "extremely narrow-minded" and argues that the rights restored to women "were given in the framework of Shariaa, which meant to honour women". However, it was only after the death of a radical cleric who had been implacably opposed to the changes that the amendments were eventually passed.

Jehan Sadat expresses concern about women losing the ground they gained two or three decades ago. She cites the examples of political representation, career opportunities and freedom of dress. Further amendment of the Personal Status Law—for example in the area of polygamy and divorce—seems unlikely. Women's groups are campaigning around issues such as an alternative marriage contract which enhances women's rights, but sociologists agree that women are coming under increasing pressure in the 1990s. While they often shoulder both male and female role responsibilities, society continues to deny them their most basic rights, including those over their own bodies, while radical religious groups want them to surrender whatever remaining freedom they have.

References

Introduction

1. Balchin, C, Mumtaz, K and Shaheed, F, *The Woman Not the Womb, Population Control vs. Women's Reproductive Rights*, Special Bulletin, March 1994, Shirkat Gah, Women's Resource Centre, Lahore, Pakistan.
2. Sinding, S, "Getting to replacement: bridging the gap between individual rights and demographic goals", in *Family Planning, Meeting Challenges: Promoting Choices*, Proceedings of the IPPF Family Planning Congress, New Delhi, October 1992, Parthenon Publishing Group, New York.
3. Sen, G, "Women's empowerment and human rights: the challenge to policy", in Graham-Smith, F (ed), *Population —The Complex Reality*, report of the Population Summit of the World's Scientific Academies, Royal Society, London, 1994.
4. Bongaarts, J, "The fertility impact of family planning programs", in *Family Planning, Meeting Challenges: Promoting Choices*, op cit; and Cleland, J, "Different pathways to demographic transition" in Graham-Smith, F (ed), *Population—The Complex Reality*, op cit.
5. Sen, G, Germain, A and Chen, L (eds), *Population Policies Reconsidered: Health, Empowerment and Rights*, Harvard University Press, Boston, 1994.
6. "Women's human rights and reproductive rights", a briefing paper prepared for the 1993 World Human Rights Conference in Vienna, Center for Reproductive Law and Policy, New York.
7. Dixon-Mueller, R and Wasserheit, J, *The Culture of Silence: Reproductive Tract Infections Among Women in the Third World*, International Women's Health Coalition, New York, 1991.
8. Wasserheit, J and Holmes, K, "Reproductive Tract Infections: challenges for international health policy, programs, and research", in Germaine, A,

Holmes, K et al (eds), *Reproductive Tract Infections, Global Impact and Priorities for Women's Reproductive Health*, Plenum Press, New York and London, 1992.
9. Ibid.
10. "Statement by the African Academy of Sciences at the Population Summit", in Graham-Smith, F (ed), *Population—The Complex Reality*, op cit; and Nandan, G, "Science academies call for zero population growth", *British Medical Journal*, Vol 307, 6 November 1993, London.
11. Ketting, E, "Global overview of abortion", in *Planned Parenthood Challenges 1993/1*, International Planned Parenthood Federation, London.
12. Ibid.
13. Zeng, Y, "Causes and implications of recent increase in the reported sex ratio at birth in China", *Population and Development Review*, Vol 19, No 2, Population Council, New York, 1993.
14. Sen, A, "Missing Women", *British Medical Journal*, Vol 304, N0 6827, 7 March 1992, pp587-588
15. Toubia, N, *Female Genital Mutilation: A Call for Global Action*, Women, Ink, New York, 1993.
16. "Brazil: Women's Reproductive Health", Report No 8215-BR, World Bank, Washington DC, 23 August 1991.
17. Chi, I-C and Thapa, S, "Postpartum tubal sterilisation: an international perspective on some programmatic issues", *Journal of Biosocial Science*, Vol 25, 1993, pp51-61.
18. Faúndes, A and Cecatti, J, "Which policy for caesarean sections in Brazil? An analysis of trends and consequences", *Health Policy and Planning*, 1993, Vol 8, No 1, Oxford University Press, Oxford, pp33-42.
19. "The prevention and treatment of obstetric fistulae", report of a Technical Working Group, Geneva, 17-21 April, 1989, WHO/FHE/89.5.20.
20. Fleming, A et al, "Growth during pregnancy in Nigerian teenage primigravidae", *British Journal of Obstetrics and Gynaecology*, 1985, Supplement 5, pp32-39.
21. Lee, E and Made, P, "Sex and the teenage girl", *Populi*, Vol 21, No 3, March 1994, UNFPA, New York.
22. Cottingham, J and Royston, E, "Obstetric Fistulae: a review of available information", WHO/MCH/MSM/91.5.
23. Clementson, D et al, "Incidence of HIV transmission with HIV-1 discordant heterosexual partnerships in Nairobi, Kenya", Abstract No 3187, 6th International Conference on AIDS, San Franciso, 1990, cited in Berer, M with Ray, S, *Women and HIV/AIDS: An International Resource Book*, Pandora, London, 1993.

The Magnitude of Neglect

1. UNICEF Survey (Tamil Nadu, Maharashtra, Jammu and Kashmir, Andhra Pradesh), January-March 1990, New Delhi (unpublished).
2. Personal communication, Dr Kantharaj, Deputy Director, State AIDS Cell, Tamil Nadu, June 1994.
3. Wasserheit, J N and Holmes, K, "RTIs: Challenges for international health policy, programs, and research" in Germain, A et al (eds), *Reproductive Tract Infections: Global Impact and Priorities for Women's Health*, Plenum Press, New York, 1992.
4. "Management of patients with sexually transmitted diseases", Technical Report Series No 810, WHO, Geneva, 1991.
5. Luthra, U K et al, "Reproductive tract infections in India: the need for comprehensive reproductive health policy and programs" in Germain, A et al (eds), op cit.
6. Wasserheit, J N and Holmes, K, op cit.
7. Luthra, U K et al, op cit.
8. Karkar, M, "Reproductive Technologies and the Third World", *Medico Circle Friends Bulletin*, Bombay, August-December 1993.
9. "Search team in Mangrol, Gujarat", *Medico Circle Friends Bulletin*, Bombay, August-December 1993.
10. Chatterjee, M and Chawla, J, "Women's Voices", *Seminar*, No 410, October 1993, New Delhi.
11. Coeytaux, F, "Abortion", in Koblinsky, M et al (eds), *The Health of Women: A Global Perspective*, Westview Press, Boulder, Colorado, 1993.
12. Bang, R A and Bang, A T, "High prevalence of gynaecological diseases in rural Indian women", *The Lancet*, Vol 1, No 8629, 14 January 1989, London, pp85-87.
13. Pyle, D F and Koblinsky, M, "Premarital sex in rural India", *The Lancet*, Vol 1, No 8640, 1 April 1989, London, p727.
14. Bang, R A and Bang, A T, op cit.
15. Chatterjee, M and Chawla, J, op cit.
16. Luthra, U K et al, op cit.
17. *Health for the Millions*, Voluntary Health Association of India, New Delhi, August 1992.
18. Chatterjee, M, "Reorienting policy", *Seminar*, No 410, October 1993, New Delhi.

In Dark Corners

1. Mpangile, G S et al, "Factors associated with induced abortion in public hospitals in Dar es Salaam, Tanzania", *Reproductive Health Matters*, No 2,

November 1993, London.
2. Ibid.
3. Mbaga, C, "Quinine [chloroquine] pills used for inducing abortions in Tanzania", *Development Forum*, March/April 1990, United Nations Department of Public Information, New York.
4. Coeytaux, F et al, "Abortion" in Koblinsky, M et al (eds), *The Health of Women: A Global Perspective*, Westview Press, Boulder, Colorado, 1993.
5. Ibid.
6. Ibid.
7. Mpangile, G S et al, op cit, p29.
8. Coeytaux, F et al, op cit.
9. Mpangile, G S et al, op cit, pp21-23.

Unwelcome Daughters

1. Zeng, Y, "Causes and implications of the recent increase in the reported sex ratio at birth in China", *Population and Development Review*, Vol 19, No 2, Population Council, New York, 1993.
2. Personal communication, Professor John Cleland, Centre for Population Studies, London, UK, July 1993.
3. Chang, K-S, "Family support systems in Korea: perceptions, conditions, and policy goals", *Impact of Fertility Decline on Population Policies and Programme Strategies*, Korea Institute for Health and Social Affairs, Seoul, 1992.
4. Ross, J and Smith, D, "Family planning directions after the demographic transition", *Impact of Fertility Decline on Population Policies and Programmes*, Korea Institute for Health and Social Affairs, Seoul, 1992.
5. Ibid.
6. "Family formation and childbirth", Korea Institute for Health and Social Affairs, Seoul, 1992.
7 Chang, K-S, op cit.
8. Ibid.
9. "Family formation and fertility behaviour in the Republic of Korea", Korea Institute for Health and Social Affairs, Seoul, 1992.
10. Byung-Hee, C, "Health and medical problems", in Bok, K (ed), *Contemporary Social Problems*, Center for Social and Cultural Studies, Seoul, 1991.
11. Ibid.
12. "Study of abortion practices and people's thinking", The Korea Criminal Policy Research Center, Seoul, 1991.
13. Im, S-Y, *Case Study of Abortion among Married Women*, Ewha Women's University, Seoul, 1990.

14. Ibid.
15. "30 years of population policy", Korea Institute for Health and Social Affairs, Seoul, 1991.
16. Ross, J and Smith, D, op cit.
17. Ibid.
18. Personal communication, Professor Kyung-Sup Chang, 8 June 1994.
19. Chang, K-S, op cit, p206.

Charity will not Liberate Women

1. Toubia, N, *Female Genital Mutilation: A Call for Action*, Women, Ink, New York, 1993.

The Oldest Contraceptive

1. Kennedy, J, "Lactation and contraception", *Ginecologia y Obstetricia de Mexico*, Vol 58 (Suppl 1), April-May 1990.
2. Perez, A et al, "Clinical study of the Lactational Amenorrhea Method for family planning", *The Lancet*, 18 April 1992, Vol 339, No 8799, London.
3. Labbok, M, "The Lactational Amenorrhea Method: Why Bother? Clinical data for policy change", paper presented at American Public Health Association, Washington DC, 8-12 November 1992.
4. Bracher, M, "Breastfeeding, lactational infecundity, contraception and the spacing of births: implications of the Bellagio Consensus statement", *Health Transition Review*, 1992, Vol 2, No 1, Canberra, Australia.
5. Kennedy, K et al, "Rejoinder to Bracher", *Health Transition Review*, 1993, Vol 3, No 1, Canberra, Australia.
6. Ibid.
7. Labbok, M, op cit.
8. Balmacéda-Gutierrez, C and Faye de Vera, A, "Litany for the last March 8 under a woman president", *Laya Feminist Quarterly*, Laya Women's Collective, March 1992, Vol 1, No 1, Manila, pp18-27.
9. "Report on breastfeeding patterns among Filipinos", Research Institute for Tropical Medicine, Department of Health, Metro Manila, 1988; similar results were reported in Popkin, B M et al, "Breastfeeding trends in the Philippines 1973 and 1983", *American Journal of Publications on Health*, 1988, No 78:32.
10 "New directions in the Philippine Family Planning Program", the Population and Human Resource Division, World Bank Regional Office for Asia, Manila, 1991.
11. Solon, O et al, "Health sector financing in the Philippines", *Health Finance Development Monograph No 2*, US Agency for International Development,

Washington DC, March 1992.
12. "New directions in the Philippine Family Planning Program", op cit.
13. Balmacéda-Gutierrez, C and Faye de Vera, A, op cit.
14. "Population policy and economic development: the Philippine experience and prospects", a speech given by Economic Planning Secretary Cielito Habito at symposium on population policy and economic development, 19-20 July 1993, Asian Development Bank, Metro Manila.
15. Danguilan, M J, *Making Choices in Good Faith: A Challenge to the Catholic Church's Teachings on Sexuality and Contraception*, WomanHealth, Quezon City, Philippines, 1993.
16. Pastoral Letter of the Catholic Bishops' Conference of the Philippines, 1993.
17. Danguilan, M J, op cit.
18. Findings of a national survey of Filipino women's attitudes towards family planning and contraceptive use, conducted by the Population Institute of the University of the Philippines, Quezon City, 1993 (publication forthcoming).
19. "New directions in the Philippine Family Planning Program", op cit.
20. Tan, M, "Facts and figures: pregnancy and childbirth in the Philippines", Women's Global Network on Reproductive Rights, Amsterdam, September-December 1988.
21. Kennedy, K et al, op cit.

Choice or Authorised Crime?

1. Data quoted in Barros, F et al, "Epidemic of caesarean sections in Brazil", *The Lancet*, Vol 338, No 8760, 20 July 1991.
2. See Barros, F et al, "Why so many caesarean sections? The need for a further policy change in Brazil", *Health Policy and Planning*, 1986, Vol 1, No 1, Oxford University Press, Oxford, pp19-29; Faúndes, A and Cecatti, J, "Which policy for caesarean sections in Brazil? An analysis of trends and consequences", *Health Policy and Planning*, 1993, Vol 8, No 1, Oxford University Press, Oxford, pp33-42; and Barros, F et al, "Epidemic of caesarean sections in Brazil", op cit.
3. Barros, F et al, "Epidemic of caesarean sections in Brazil", op cit.
4. Faúndes, A and Cecatti, J, "Which policy for caesarean sections in Brazil? An analysis of trends and consequences", op cit, pp33-42.
5. Ibid.
6. Ibid.
7. Ibid.
8. "Brazil: Women's Reproductive Health", Report No 8215-BR, World

Bank, Washington DC, 23 August 1991.
9. Faúndes, A and Cecatti, J, op cit, pp33-42.
10. Barros, F et al, "Epidemic of caesarean sections in Brazil", op cit.
11. "Brazil: Women's Reproductive Health", op cit.
12. Berquó, E, "Brazil, um caso examplar: anticoncepção e partos cirúrgicos", Cebrap/UNICAMP, Campinas, 1993.
13. *Third World Guide 91/92*, Third World Institute, Montevideo, Uruguay.
14. "Brazil: Women's Reproductive Health", op cit.
15. Bahamondes, L, "Significado do recente aumento do número de solicitantes de reversão de laquedura", *Femina*, Vol 20, 1992.
16. "Research on family health in Northeast Brazil", BEMFAM-DHS, 1991.
17. Pollack, A, "Male and female sterilisation: long-term health consequences", *Outlook*, Vol 11, No 1, Seattle, March 1993.
18. Hardy, E et al, "Avaliação do Programa de Assistência Integral à Saúde da Mulher no Estado de São Paulo. Resultados da Area Metropolitana e do Interior do Estado. Informações Relativas ao Pre-Natal, Parto e Revisão Pós-parto", CEMICAMP, Campinas, 1988.
19. Chi, I-C, and Thapa, S, "Postpartum tubal sterilisation: an international perspective on some programmatic issues", *Journal of Biosocial Science*, Vol 25, 1993, pp51-61.
20. Berquó, E, op cit.
21. "Fertility and family planning in Latin America: Challenges of the 1990s", Population Reference Bureau, Washington DC, June 1992.

To See Her Smile

1. Ministry of Health, Accra.
2. *Annual Report*, Maternal Child Health/Family Planning Departments, Ministry of Health, Accra, 1992.
3. Ministry of Health, Accra.

The Silent Shame

1. Quoted in Cottingham, J and Royston, E, "Obstetric Fistulae: a review of available information", WHO, Geneva, WHO/MCH/MSM/91.5.
2. Cottingham, J and Royston E, op cit.
3. Obituary for Reginald Hamlin, *The Times*, London, 14 August 1993.
4. Cottingham, J and Royston, E, op cit.
5. Personal communication, Dr John Kelly, 7 January 1994.
6. AbouZahr, C and Royston, E (compilers), *Maternal Mortality: A Global Factbook*, WHO, Geneva, 1991.
7. *Human Development Report 1994*, UNDP, Oxford University Press.

8. Toubia, N, *Female Genital Mutilation: A Call for Global Action*, Women, Ink, New York, 1993.
9. Kelly, J and Kwast, B, "Epidemiologic study of vesicovaginal fistulas in Ethiopia", *International Urogynecology Journal*, No 4, 1993.
10. Personal communication, 10 November 1993.

Double Standard, Double Threat

1. Brown, T and Sittitrai, W, "The Impact of HIV on Children in Thailand", unpublished manuscript, Save the Children Fund (UK), 1992.
2. Linter, B and Panos, "Asia's AIDS crossroads?", *WorldAIDS*, No 28, July 1993, Panos, London.
3. Lorsomboon, P et al, "A survey on the prevalence of HIV-1 among the well-off population admitted into private hospitals in Bangkok" in *Excerpts from Studies [Social and Behavioural Issues]*, presented at 3rd National AIDS Conference, Bangkok, July 1993, Ministry of Public Health (Thailand) and WHO.
4. Brown, T and Sittirai, W, op cit.
5. Epidemiology Division, Ministry of Public Health, Bangkok, December 1993.
6. Usher, A D, "After the forest: AIDS as ecological collapse in Thailand", *Development Dialogue*, 1992:1-2, Dag Hammarskjöld Foundation, Uppsala.
7. Clements, A, "Thailand stifles AIDS campaign", *British Medical Journal*, London, Vol 304, No 6837, 16 May 1992.
8. Chaikuna, A and Boonrapa, V, "Attitudes and Aids", in *Excerpts from Studies [Social Anthropology and Behavioural Issues]*, op cit.
9. Uraiwan, U et al, "Sexual experience and condom use among Thai male teenagers" in *Excerpts from Studies [Social Anthropology and Behavioural Issues]*, op cit.
10. Ungphakorn, J, "The impact of AIDS on women in Thailand", in Berer, M, with Ray, S, *Women and HIV/AIDS: An International Resource Book*, Pandora, London, 1993.
11 Figures from the Department of Communicable Disease Control, Ministry of Public Health, Bangkok.
12. "Statistics Report", Department of Communicable Disease Control, Ministry of Public Health, Bangkok, 1993.
13. Smith, D, "'Green cards' for Thai sex workers", *WorldAIDS*, No 10, July 1992, Panos, London.
14. Figures from the Duang Prateep Foundation and the AIDS Project of the Thai Red Cross Society, 1992.
15. Clementson, D et al, "Incidence of HIV transmission within HIV-1 discordant heterosexual partnerships in Nairobi, Kenya", Abstract No

3187, 6th International Conference on AIDS, San Francisco, 1990, cited in Berer, M with Ray, S, *Women and HIV/AIDS: An International Resource Book*, op cit, p118.

Room to Decide

1. Floro, M and Wolf, J, "The economic and social impacts of girls' primary education in developing countries", US Agency for International Development, Office of Education and Women in Development, Washington DC, 1990.
2. Sathar, Z, Crook, N, Callum, C and Kazi, S, "Women's status and fertility change in Pakistan", *Population and Development Review*, Population Council, Vol 14, No 3, September 1988.
3. Sathar, Z and Kazi, S, "Female employment and fertility: further investigation of an ambivalent association", *The Pakistan Development Review: An International Journal of Development Economics*, Vol 28, No 3, Autumn 1989.
4. Manzoor, K, "Female status and its impact on reproductive behaviour in Pakistan", paper presented at the 9th AGM of the Pakistan Society of Development Economists, 7-10 January 1993, National Institute of Population Studies, Islamabad.
5. "Women's human rights and reproductive rights", a briefing paper prepared for the 1993 World Human Rights Conference in Vienna, Center for Reproductive Law and Policy, New York.

We Can't Stop Now

1. *Human Development Report 1993*, UNDP, Oxford University Press.
2. Grant, J, *The State of the World's Children*, United Nations Children's Fund (UNICEF), Oxford University Press, 1993.
3. *Statistical Pocket Book of Pakistan*, Federal Bureau of Statistics, Islamabad, 1992.
4. Grant, J, *The State of the World's Children*, op cit.
5. *Newsline*, Karachi, 15 January 1994.
6. Ibid.
7. Husain, R and Ispahani, A, "Interview with Nafis Sadik", *Newsline*, Karachi, January 1993.
8. *The State of Human Rights in Pakistan*, Human Rights Commission of Pakistan, Islamabad, 1993.
9. Shah, N, "Feudal landlords lock women in purdah", *Panoscope*, Panos, London, No 35, April 1993.
10. "The woman or the womb", *South Asia*, Islamabad, 24-30 January 1994.

11. *Pakistan Health and Demographic Survey 1992-1993*, National Institute of Population Studies, Islamabad; Grant, J, *The State of the World's Children*, op cit.
12. *Pakistan Population Review*, National Institute of Population Studies, Islamabad, Spring 1991.
13. Arif, K, *Dawn Economic Review*, Karachi, 19 January 1994.
14. Saaed, H, "Can Pakistan's population programme move forward?" *National Health*, January-March 1994, Karachi, p29.

Rites and Rights

1. "Unholy struggle with third-world genie", *The Lancet*, 21 August 1993, Vol 342, No 8869, London.
2. Information from Dr Claudia Garcia Moreno, former Medical Officer, Oxfam, UK.
3. "Inquietan a obispos corrientes que propician aborto y divorcio", *El Mercurio*, Santiago, 23 November 1993.
4. "Terrorismo demográfico", *El Mercurio*, Santiago, 26 November 1993.
5. Kissling, F, "Reproductive Rites and Wrongs", *Populi*, New York, July/August 1992, p15.
6. Quoted in "Una lectura feminista de los textos de Santo Domingo", *Conciencia Latinoamericana*, Montevideo, Uruguay, July/August/September 1993, p9.
7. "Iglesia rechaza consumismo y legalización del divorcio", *El Mercurio*, Santiago, 27 November 1993.
8. "Programa de educación al amor y sexualidad", Comisión Nacional de Pastoral Familiar (Chilean Bishops' Conference), May 1992, Santiago.
9. *Noticias Aliadas*, Lima, 21 October 1993.
10. "No todos los hijos son iguales", *El Mercurio*, Santiago, 26 September 1993.
11. Valenzuela, S, "Los adolescentes chilenos", unpublished paper presented at the seminar "Sexualidad, Reproducción y Servicios de Salud: Hacia la Construcción de Derechos", Corporación de Salud y Politícas Sociales (CORSAPS), November 1993.
12. Iturriaga, M A et al, *Madres Solteras: Análisis de una Experiencia*, Ediciones Primus Ltda, Santiago, 1993.
13. Information from Dr B Viel, the Chilean Family Planning Association.
14. Requena, M (ed), *Aborto Inducido en Chile*, Edición Sociedad Chilena de Salud Pública, Santiago, 1990.
15. "Situación de la salud de la mujer en Chile", Facultad Latinoamericana de Ciencias Sociales (FLASCO)/Corporación de Salud y Politicas Sociales (CORSAPS), 1991.

16. Information from Professor Mónica Weisner, University of Chile, September 1993.
17. Cruz-Coke, M and Campos, E, *Mujeres Chilenas 1992*, Centro de Estudios de la Realidad Contemporánea (CERC).
18. Quoted by Weisner, M, "Comportamiento reproductivo y aborto inducido en mujeres chilenas de sectores populares: una perspectiva antropológica", in Requena, M (ed), *Aborto Inducido en Chile*, Edicion Sociedad Chilena de Salud Pública, Santiago, 1990.
19. Valdés, T, *Venid, Benditas de mi Padre: los pobladoras, sus rutinas y sus sueños*, FLASCO, Santiago, 1988.
20. Valdés, T, "Vida cotidiana, subjetividad y reproducción", paper presented at CORSAPS seminar "Sexualidad, Reproducción y Servicios de Salud: Hacia la Construcción de Derechos", Santiago, 10 November 1993.

In the Shadow of a Man
1. Research by the Association for Combating Unhealthy Practices, Cairo.
2. Khattab, H A S, *The Silent Endurance: Social conditions of women's reproductive health in rural Egypt*, UNICEF/Population Council (regional offices), 1992. Available from UNICEF, Amman, Jordan.
3. Mahran, M, *The Population Problem in Egypt*, Ministry of Population and Family Welfare, Cairo, 1994.
4. Khattab, H A S, op cit.